Dachau Liberated

The Official Report

by

U.S. Seventh Army

Released Within Days of the Camp's Liberation by
Elements of the 42nd and 45th Divisions

Edited by

Michael W. Perry

Inkling Books   Seattle   2000

This book is based on a report originally published under the title *Dachau* in May of 1945 by the U.S. Seventh Army in Germany. It has been retitled *Dachau Liberated: The Official Report* and contains all of the original report plus additional editorial material by Michael W. Perry and sketches made at Dachau on April 30, 1945 by then 2nd Lt. Ted Mackechnie.

The text of this book is derived from the original, typewritten edition of *Dachau* printed by the 649th Engr Topo Battalion of the U.S. Seventh Army. (There is a reproduction of its cover on the title page.) This edition contains all the text, photographs and illustrations of the original and follows that report exactly except for minor typographical corrections and changes noted in square brackets. (Of necessity, the placement of graphics differs from the original.) The editorial material in this book is new and has never been published before. The penciled sketches are included with the permission of Ted Mackechnie.

Library Cataloging Data

U.S. Seventh Army
Dachau Liberated: The Official Report
Edited by Perry, Michael W. (Wiley)
111 p. 23 cm.
Includes 35 illustrations, 4 appendices, footnotes and an index
ISBN: 1-58742-0031 (paper)
LC: 00-105121
1. Germany 2. Nazism 3. Concentration camps 4. Dachau 5. Auschwitz 6. Hoess, Rudolf 7.World War II 8. U.S. Seventh Army 9. Perry, Michael W. (editor)
Keywords: Germany, Nazism, Concentration camp, Dachau, Auschwitz, Hoess, Rudolf, Medical experimentation, Holocaust
D805.G3 U57 2000
940.54
Published in the United States of America on acid-free paper.
First Inkling Edition: July 2000
Internet: http://www.inklingbooks.com/

Contents

Dachau from the Air

Editor: These photographs of the camp were taken on May 27, 1945 by
1st Lt. Harold L. Valentine of the 163rd Signal Photographic Company.

Foreword

Dachau, 1933–1945, will stand for all time as one of history's most gruesome symbols of inhumanity. There our troops found sights, sounds, and stenches horrible beyond belief, cruelties so enormous as to be incomprehensible to the normal mind. Dachau and death were synonymous.

No words or pictures can carry the full impact of these unbelievable scenes, but this report presents some of the outstanding facts and photographs in order to emphasize the type of crime which elements of the SS committed thousands of times a day, to remind us of the ghastly capabilities of certain classes of men, to strengthen our determination that they and their works shall vanish from the earth.

The sections comprising this report were prepared by the agencies indicated. They remain substantially as they were originally submitted in the belief that to consolidate this material in a single literary style would seriously weaken its realism.

WILLIAM W. QUINN
COLONEL, G.S.C.
A C OF S, G-2
7TH U.S. ARMY

Credits

Composition—Major Alfred L. Howes, G-2 Sect., 7th Army

Art Work—T/Sgt. John S. Denney, G-2 Sect., 7th Army

Copy Preparation—T/3 Chas W. Denney, Jr., G-2 Sect., 7th Army

Photographs—163d Signal Photo Company

Printing—649th Engr Topo Battalion

Editor's Preface

For some, April 29, 1945 is a day that will remain forever etched in their minds. For it was on that day that elements of the U.S. Seventh Army liberated the Nazi concentration camp at Dachau. This book is their story, told in their own words, and published within days of the camp's liberation.

The war was clearly over. That very morning in an underground Berlin bunker, Hitler was dictating his last will and political testament. The next day he would commit suicide, ending after twelve the Reich that he said would last a thousand years. As they awoke that Sunday morning, many American troops had one thought foremost in their minds—surviving the war so they could go home. But when they went to sleep that evening, their lives had been deeply affected. Disturbing thoughts now flooded their minds.

We will never know all the events of that day. What Winston Churchill aptly termed the "fog of war" has forever obscured exactly what happened. Soldiers focused on staying alive in combat do not take notes of events.

We do know that two divisions, the 42nd and 45th Infantry, were spearheading the Seventh Army's drive toward Munich and acutely conscious that the Wehrmacht might make a last desperate stand before the city. It was then that they stumbled upon a camp whose existence and purpose had been unknown to many of them.

The 42nd, nicknamed the "Rainbow Division" would enter the camp from the inmates' barracks on the east side. The 45th or "Thunderbirds" would enter from the west side where the camp's SS guards were housed. Odd as it sounds, while many camps guards either fled or willingly surrendered, others fought on to the very last, defending their long-held 'right' to terrorize the camp's thirty-thousand inmates. Most disturbing of all, inmates would continue to be shot for trying to escape even as the camp was being liberated.

Over the years, many of those soldiers have retained a special attachment to the camp, to its survivors, and to a belief that what happened there must never happen again. That belief was shared by those who followed them into the camp on succeeding days. One of those soldiers, Ted Mackechnie, has kindly given permission to include here sketches he made on the day following the liberation. Though not part of the original edition of this book, their inclusion is appropriate. Shortly after the camp's liberation, they were published in his division newspaper, *Rainbow Reveille*.

For many of the soldiers who stumbled onto the camp that day, their first glimpse into its horrors came as they walked along a rail spur outside the camp. Crammed into railroad cars and scattered along the tracks were the bodies of men who had been alive when they had begun the long journey during which their captors fully expected them to die of thirst and starvation. At the end of that journey, Dachau's crematory stood eagerly waiting.

Coming closer, the soldiers saw the towers and high-voltage fences that kept the inmates confined to their man-made hell. From this particular tower, lettered B, several guards with machine guns fought American troops in one last, desperate attempt to maintain their reign of terror.

As with Auschwitz, articles of clothing were often all that remained of inmates whose bodies had been consumed by the flames. This sketch is of a pile of clothing stored under an awning just outside the crematory.

Perhaps the grimmest of all Mackechnie's sketches is this, made of a room which served as a holding area next to the crematory. When disease, shooting and incoming transports were at their peak, people often died too quickly to be burned—two at a time—by five ovens that ran around the clock. According to Mackechnie, after one American soldier saw this room he whispered that it was, "Like a maniac's woodpile." These are the disturbing images that soldiers of the U.S. Seventh Army still retain from a half century ago.

For many of Dachau's inmates, a crematory oven would be their last stop. After every bit of labor had been extracted from their malnourished bodies, they were of no more use to their captors. Some would left to die of starvation and disease. Others would meet a speedier end at the *Schiesstand* near the crematory. In haste, some would be buried in mass graves, but most came to the crematory whose flames burned around the clock.

This edition is dedicated to all those whose lives were forever altered on that day in April of 1945. May it help us to never forget what happened at Dachau.

MICHAEL W. PERRY
SEATTLE, JULY 5, 2000

1

Camp Organization

It was the familiar Nazi technique of indirect rule....
When this stage was reached where prisoners persecuted
fellow prisoners instead of preserving a sense of common
solidarity, the success of the SS method of control was, of
course, complete.... That so many formerly genuine political prisoners succumbed to this pressure and sank to a
criminal level of existence was one of the real tragedies in
places like Dachau.

Summary

At Dachau the only objective of the inmates was to survive
under the most primitive and cruel conditions which constantly threatened their sanity and physical existence. Little
more than this was humanly possible. As a result of these
abnormal conditions, this camp of 30,000 men cannot be
compared to the structure of any normal society differenti-
ated by social classes, political, religious, or professional affiliations. Hence, neither normal moral standards nor normal
political or sociological criteria are applicable to the Dachau
situation.

The inmates of the camp did not act as members of their
former social class or as representatives of political or religious groups—whether they were professional men, workers, intellectuals, Communists, nationalists, Catholics, or
Protestants—but only as human beings in a struggle for survival against starvation and mass murders. This was true as
much of the minority of those who took charge of the internal
organization of the camp under the SS as of the majority of

those who did not.

Living under these abnormal conditions, the inmates, especially those who had gained a position of some power and security, were frequently degraded and degenerated to a criminal level, copying the methods and practices of the SS for their own protection and benefit. Because so many of the administrative positions were held by German prisoners, rather strong anti-German sentiments developed among the non-German inmates of the camp.

The only form of self-organization among the prisoners took place within the framework of the internal organization of the camp. The "Labor Allocation Office" (*Arbeitseinsatz*) and its subsidiary branches was the key agency which was successively in the hands of different cliques who frequently abused their position of power for the sake of personal advantages. These groups were composed largely of Germans until the last six months.

Otherwise, the level of existence in the camp together with the insidious system of internal controls, whereby prisoners themselves were placed in the service of the SS, did not permit the emergence of any organizational form. There was no underground organization or political activity in the accepted sense of the word. Even expressions of mutual help and solidarity among members of the same national group never transcended the level of personal relations between people bound by friendships, common background, and language. They never took the form of organized action.

Only during the last phase of the camp, an organizational network was set up between leading representatives of various nationalities which led to the formation of the "International Prisoners Committee"—today the highest authority in the camp. This Committee was concerned entirely with matters of self-help in preparation of the eventual liberation of the camp. It has never been dominated by any political program or orientation.

This report is based on two days' investigation of conditions in the Dachau Concentration Camp. It does not intend to give either an exhaustive history of the camp or a comprehensive survey of all aspects of camp life. Numerous reports are in the process of being written which, when completed, will give a full picture of the Dachau Concentration Camp. This report is concerned primarily with one aspect of life in Dachau: the internal organization of the camp, the evidence of self-administration among the prisoners, and the emergence of special control and pressure groups, as well as the position of the various social, political, and national groups within this organizational framework.

History

Dachau is the oldest Nazi concentration camp. It was set up in March 1933 and constructed to house a maximum of between 8,000–10,000 prisoners. It was designed to serve as a camp for German political prisoners and Jews. Early 1935, however, the first criminal prisoners arrived in the camp and, ever since then, the camp has included a small minority of criminal prisoners. The original number of inmates grew substantially in 1937 after the German annexation of Austria and Czechoslovakia.[1] During the war the prisoner body was further increased steadily through the influx of political and military prisoners from the occupied territories and through numerous transports arriving from other German concentration camps. The first Polish prisoners arrived in 1940, to be followed in 1941 by prisoners from the Balkan countries, and in 1942 by the first Russian prisoners. Throughout this period the camp also absorbed a large number of prisoners from the occupied Western countries, especially France.

While the total number of inmates fluctuated—owing to incoming and outgoing transports and the systematic policy

---

1. Editor: This should read 1938. Austria was annexed on 12 March 1938, and the infamous Munich Agreement giving Hitler the Czechoslovakian Sudetenland was concluded at the end of September that same year. Accomplishments such as these were why *Time* magazine proclaimed Hitler "Man of the Year" for 1938.

of extermination in the camp—it was generally, during the war, between 22,000 to 30,000; roughly three times the maximum capacity of the camp. It reached its peak sometime in 1944, when numerous transports arrived from the evacuated concentration camps in the East (e.g., Auschwitz), the West (e.g., Natzweiler) and inside Germany. Dachau then held more than 60,000 prisoners and included an entire network of smaller subsidiary camps located in its immediate surroundings. These over-crowded conditions were largely responsible for the subsequent increase in the death rate at the camp. Aside from the official murders by the SS, thousands and thousands of prisoners died during the fall and winter of 1944 from starvation and typhus.

Shortly before the camp was liberated, the Nazis sent out a large transport of special prisoners, consisting chiefly of Russians, Poles, Germans, and Jews. The Nazis also evacuated the so-called "honorary prisoners" (*Ehrenhaeftlinge*), i.e., the famous political and religious hostages they held at Dachau (Niemoeller, Schuschnigg, Daladier, Blum, etc.).[2] Plans to destroy the entire camp were apparently foiled at the last moment. At the time of liberation there were about 32,000 prisoners left in Dachau. The daily rate of people dying of exhaustion, starvation, and typhus was about 200. It is now between 50 to 80.

Composition

The inmates of Dachau can be classified according to two categories: (a) by nationality, (b) by the type of crime of which

---

2. Editor: Martin Niemoeller was an orthodox Lutheran pastor who led the anti-Nazi Confessing Church. He was arrested on July 1, 1937 and kept in various prisons and concentration camps until the war's end. Kurt von Schuschnigg was Austria's chancellor from 1934 to 1938. He fought desperately to prevent his country's annexation by Germany. Édouard Daladier was France's Premier at the time of the German invasion. Prosecuted by the Vichy French government, he was handed over to the Germans for imprisonment. Léon Blum was France's first Jewish Premier (1936–37) and like Daladier a critic of the Vichy regime. All survived the war, in part because their imprisonment prevented them from being involved in the July 1944 plot to kill Hitler and the bloodbath unleashed on those who were.

they were accused. The differentiation by nationalities, of course, only arose during the war when the camp began to include different national groups. Before the war the number of foreigners was insignificant. German, Austrian, and Jewish prisoners represented the numerically strongest groups.

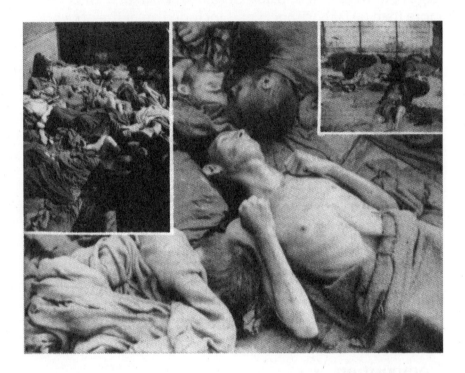

During the war, the Germans and Austrians became a numerical minority. The numerically strongest national group were the Poles, followed by the Russians, French, Yugoslavs, Germans, Jews, and Czechs. A rough estimate at 1 May 1945 gives the following statistical break-down: Poles: 9,200; Russians: 3,900; French: 3,700; Yugoslavs: 3,200; Jews: 2,100; Czechoslovaks: 1,500; Germans: 1,000; and a number of other national groups (Belgians, Hungarians, Italians, Austrians, Greeks, etc.) below 1,000.[3] The average number of Germans held here during the war, however, was about 3,000. Some two thousand Germans were evacuated and killed in

3. Editor: For more precise figures, see Appendix D.

the last big transport a few days before our occupation of Dachau.

Although it was the practice of the camp management to keep the various national groups mixed up with each other, members of the different nationalities always retained a natural sense of belongingness, solidarity and group-feeling.

The prisoners were further divided according to the type of crime of which they were found guilty, indicated by differently coloured patches worn on their uniforms or work-clothes. The most important patches were the red ones identifying political prisoners, the green identifying criminal prisoners, and the black identifying "asocial" elements, i.e., people who had violated labor regulations, committed sabotage, etc. There were numerous other patches (pink, purple, yellow) identifying other crimes. Prisoners of war sent to Dachau were treated and designated as political prisoners.

As far as the prisoners themselves are concerned, the camp was divided sharply only between two groups: the "reds" or political prisoners and the "greens" or criminal prisoners. The SS tried to break down this distinction by an ingenious system of creating a "prisoners' elite," composed of both "reds" and "greens," which assumed power over the internal organization of Dachau, controlled and frequently terrorized the camp in the name of the SS, but formally independent of the SS. This system of internal organization will be discussed in the following section. However, despite this organization of internal corruption and terror, by which the SS exercised its control indirectly, the mass of political prisoners continued to live in sharp separation from and opposition to the "criminals" and most of the prisoner bosses whom they despised, feared and hated.

It is impossible to classify prisoners according to any

other category—either by social status, class, background, or by previous political and religious affiliations. These factors dividing people in a normal type of society are totally inapplicable to the situation at Dachau where people lived the most abnormal kind of existence imaginable. Regardless of origin, education, wealth, politics, or religion, people living in Dachau for a certain time were gradually reduced to the most primitive and cruel form of existence—motivated almost exclusively by fear of death. They no longer acted as former bankers, workers, priests, Communists, intellectuals or artists, but primarily as individuals trying to survive in the physical conditions of Dachau, i.e., trying to escape the constantly threatening death by starvation, freezing, or execution. Some may still have thought of themselves in terms of their former social and political background or labels; but it is important to ask to what extent those old social labels determined their actions during the time of their imprisonment at Dachau. As far as we could ascertain, these factors are completely irrelevant for explaining the behavior of the inmates of Dachau. Living conditions in the camp were such that all former professional, social and political distinctions were gradually obliterated. People still behaved differently, some well and courageously, others evil and cruelly; but these differences cannot be derived from or identified with their former social labels (whether aristocratic, military, intellectual, or proletarian), but simply reflect the different personal reactions of individuals to a situation in which all are reduced to the most primitive social level of a struggle for mere physical survival.

Organization

The organization of the camp was based on the system of indirect rule. There were two separate spheres of controls: (a) the external control apparatus of the SS Guards, (b) the internal control organization in the hands of the prisoners themselves.

The organization of the SS Guards is comparatively unimportant. It followed the regular pattern of this paramilitary outfit. The key positions seem to have been the "camp commandant," [*Lager Kommandant*] in charge of the entire SS establishment Dachau, next the SS leader, in charge of the labor gangs and transports (*Arbeitseinsatzfuehrer*), and finally the position of the intelligence officer (*Vernehmungsfuehrer*) of the Political Division [Department], in charge of security, discipline, and punishment.[4]

These men, however, and their subordinates exercised hardly any direct control whatsoever. Instead, they used as instruments for their rule the internal organization of the camp in the hands of the prisoners themselves. This internal organization of the prisoners followed the regular pattern of a Nazi hierarchical regime. It was headed by a camp senior (*Lageraeltester*); under the camp senior there were (a) the secretary (*Lagerschreiber*) and his staff, in charge of the records, (b) the chief of police (*Polizeifuehrer*) and the camp police (*Lagerpolizei*), and the Chief of the Labor Allocation Office (*Arbeitseinsatz*) and his staff, in charge of all aspects of work performed inside and outside the camp. The Labor Office sent out the "work details" (*Arbeits Kommandos*) of which

---

4. Editor: For more on the camp's organization, see Appendices B and C.

there were about 160, each headed by a foreman called the *Capo*. Together with the camp senior these agencies and their chiefs formed the central authority of the camp.

The camp was further divided into "blocks" (*Blocks*) and "cells" (*Stuben*). And each block and each cell, in turn, had its "senior" and "secretary," called *Blockaeltester* (*Stubenaeltester*) and *Blockschreiber* (*Stubenschreiber*) respectively.

This system of internal controls served the interests of the SS most effectively. In order to deal with the enormous number of prisoners, they only had to deal through the men of the central authority to whom the subsidiary camp authorities were responsible. The SS issued general orders; the particulars of carrying these orders out were left to the internal organization of the prisoners.

It was the familiar Nazi technique of indirect rule. To guard against sabotage under this set-up, the SS at Dachau, as everywhere else, employed its own systems of prisoner spies and informants inside the camp and applied the most ruthless forms of terror whenever necessary. As agents, the SS made particular use of the minority of criminal prisoners (about 700)—sometimes disguised by red patches as political prisoners.

Under these conditions it is evident that to be part of the camp administration afforded the best possible means of survival. In an official position the individual enjoyed not only a certain sense of personal power and security, but could also negotiate deals which brought him and his friends certain small privileges in work, food, clothing, and living conditions. Hence, the struggle for survival in the camp, to the extent that it was manifested in overt actions, frequently took the form of fighting for power through the camp administration. In this process, of course, certain groups emerged among the political prisoners who seized positions of control and exploited them for their own personal benefit and for that of members of their group. Moreover, in an atmosphere, filled with terror, fear, threats, starvation and death, many of the old legitimate political prisoners themselves became corrupted and degenerated to the level of the criminals, i.e., used the brutal, criminal methods of the SS and the "greens."

There are numerous reports about thefts, beatings, and killings by political *Capos* in different positions. When this stage was reached where prisoners persecuted fellow prisoners instead of preserving a sense of common solidarity, the success of the SS method of control was, of course, complete. However, it would be incorrect, as pointed out above, to identify these groups with any social or political label. Even when they abused their power to the excess of criminal activities, they never acted as representatives of a definite social or political group, but merely as people who, having succeeded in seizing a position of limited power, exploited this position for personal advantages and favors. That so many formerly genuine political prisoners succumbed to this pressure and sank to a criminal level of existence was one of the real tragedies in places like Dachau.

Groupings of Prisoners

Labor Allocation Office

Of all the administrative agencies within the internal organization of the camps, the Labor Allocation Office (*Arbeitseinsatz*) was the key office. This office allocated the labor requirements for the different "work commandos" (*Arbeitskommandos*) and also determined the composition of the transports which were shipped out from Dachau. Both functions were of the highest importance insofar as the nature of work frequently determined one's means of subsistence (e.g., agricultural workers were generally better fed and could smuggle food back into the camp) and insofar as transports were greatly feared since their destination was generally unknown. To the extent that the prisoners had any voice or pressure on their use and disposition, this was exercised through the labor office.

The office was run entirely by prisoners. The staff consisted of a chief, several assistants and a group of clerks. The office maintained files which contained all personal data pertinent to the allocation of individuals for work of various kinds. The three main sources of employment at Dachau were (a) work inside the camp, (b) work at the SS camp, (c) work on farms and in factories in the area. The lists of people to be shipped off on transports was usually compiled from those prisoners who were not part of a regular 'Working Commando.'

In operation, the SS Labor Leader (*Arbeitseinsatzfuehrer*) simply informed the chief of the Labor Office to have a certain number of men ready at a certain time for work or for shipment on a transport. The selection of the men for any given assignment was largely left to the Labor Office itself, which drew up its lists in consultation with the block and cell seniors. It would be easy, however, to exaggerate the extent to which the Labor Office enjoyed freedom of action in these decisions. In many matters, especially in the cases of transports which were politically important, the SS office would hand down a list of people whom it wished to have included in the assignment.

Nevertheless, the positions in the Labor Office and the subsidiary command over the 'work commandos' afforded sufficient power to serve as an incentive for individuals and groups to seize these positions and defend them against outsiders. Historically, these groups were Germans simply because Germans were the oldest inhabitants of the camp. As far as we could trace the developments back, some kind of a group or clique seems to have first formed in 1937 under an Austrian Socialist by the name of Brenner. The 'Brenner Group' in the Labor Office included both German and Austrian Socialists. After the release of Brenner, it was superseded by a combination of German Socialists and Communists under a certain Kuno Rieke (Socialist) and a certain Julius Schaetzle (Communist). This combination and their staff were in control of the Labor Office until June 1944, when Schaetzle was suspected of conspiratorial activities and shipped off in a transport. Rieke died shortly thereafter in the camp. A temporary regime succeeded the Rieke-Schaetzle group until September 1944, when a new regime gradually took over, eliminating all Germans from positions of influence in the Labor Office. This last group, composed primarily of Alsatians, Lorrainers, French, Luxembourgers, Belgians, and Poles, is still in charge of the Labor Office today.

None of these groups can be considered as underground; none of them represented a political body. There was no evidence that these people acted as members of a political group with a definite political program or purpose. These men held together in their own small group or clique for the personal advantages their position offered them in the generally miserable conditions of the camp. This is not to say that they did not try to take care of friends. But the favors they could dispense were on such a personal basis and on such a low level of small physical improvements that they could never form the basis for any organized activity or relationship. It was simply part of the living conditions in the camp and part of the control system set up by the SS which placed certain of the groups of prisoners in positions of minor power. And these same factors were equally responsible for the degeneration of many of these men to a level of criminal activity against their own fellow-prisoners. Since Germans, being the oldest inmates, had generally seized control of most of the positions of influence in the administrative apparatus in the camp, the other national groups naturally developed distrust, antagonism, and frequently intense hatred of these German prisoners.

Other Posts of Control

The Germans, however, were not alone in charge of all the leading positions. The key post of the camp senior, for instance, was held by a certain Melazarian, an Armenien [Armenian] and former Red Army officer; and many of the block and cell senior as well as the 'Capos' of the 'work commandos' were chosen from different nationalities. Melazarian had so completely sold out to the SS and was so generally hated by all the inmates of the camp that he was almost beaten to death after occupation and finally executed by American troops. The same fate befell the German chief of the camp police, a certain Wernicke. But even the generally rather strong feelings against Germans are not universal, for in place of Melazarian, who was dismissed before our occupation, a certain Oskar Mueller was appointed 'camp senior.' Although a German and a former Communist, Mueller enjoys the respect and admiration of the representatives of all national groups. At present he is also a member of the International Prisoners' Committee, to be discussed below. But as in the case of the people who abused their position of power, so in the case of Mueller who did not. His former political views, as he himself stressed, have nothing to do with his present activities in the camp. He has performed his functions for the benefit of all the inmates in the camp in order to save what can humanly be saved under the disastrous conditions of life in Dachau without any other aim or motivation.

National Groups

There was no organized activity in the camp in any other form. Even the national groups which formed more or less natural divisions in the camp did not develop any organizational form. Bonds between prisoners speaking the same language and possessing the same national background naturally existed; but these personal bonds did not result in any organizational expression or in overt activities of any sort. Men of the same nationality stuck together in order to preserve their sanity and to prolong their physical existence. In the course of time, however, certain natural leaders emerged out of these national groups and these unofficially recognized leaders within the various nationalities, in turn, were eventually responsible for the only real organization which has existed in Dachau; the International Prisoners' Committee, which is the highest prisoner authority in the camp today. There were no 'international' relations on the basis of common political or social grouping. For example, no kind of unifying element seemed to exist between Russian and German Communists, or between French and Polish Catholics. Nor did people of any one national group seem to show any marked preference for members of their own social class or political affiliation as distinguished from compatriots with a different social or political background. This indifference clearly showed the levelling influence of life under the primitive, dangerous conditions of Dachau which gradually blurred all former sociological and political distinctions.

International Prisoners' Committee (IPC)

When American troops entered Dachau on the evening of 30 April they found an International Prisoners' Committee (IPC) functioning in the camp.[5] The IPC was in complete control of the camp. Most of the SS Guards had fled together with most of those prisoner elements who had cooperated with the SS and had themselves been guilty of maltreatment and murder of fellow-inmates.

The origins of the IPC go back to sometime in September of last year when Allied military successes in the West promised the possibility of an early liberation of the prisoners. A small group of inmates employed in the camp hospital served as a nucleus for the IPC: an Albanian (Kuci), a Pole (Nazewski), a Belgian (Haulet [Haulot]), and a British-Canadian (O'Leary). They established contact with representatives of other nationalities, Russian, French, etc., and also cooperated with one German, the above-mentioned Mueller, who was a recent arrival in the camp. Aside from Mueller, the "hospital nucleus" of the future IPC did not work with any German prisoners. They were too much afraid of the spies working among the Germans.

The aims of this group were simple, They wished to prepare for the advance of the Americans, save as many lives as possible in the last critical phase before liberation, and keep a record of criminal SS activities and personalities. In this program they seem to have been quite successful. Since last December they tried to keep certain key inmates as "patients" in the camp hospital where they enjoyed a certain protection. They likewise enlisted the help of a great number

---

5. Editor: American troops actually reached the camp on the afternoon of April 29.

of block and cell seniors to control the activities of criminal elements among the prisoners and to nip in the bud any provocative action which the SS might use to unloosen mass massacres. They prepared lists of crimes and criminals among the SS and their prisoner stooges. Finally, they tried to keep informed about the advance of the Allies, listening to foreign broadcasts, and spread[ing] the news by their men throughout the camp. When American troops were near Augsburg, they even established contact through prisoners working on farms in that area.

The building up of this rather closely-knit network of activities was facilitated by the gradual disintegration of SS controls during the last months, the replacement of old SS Guards, the comparatively small number of guards toward the end (about 250), and confusion created by orders and counter-orders from higher headquarters. In the last days before liberation, the IPC came practically out into the open. On 27 April, for example, a large transport of 6,700 Russians, Poles, Germans, and Jews was scheduled to leave the camp. By changing national identity patches and padding the camp records, 1,000 Russians were "hidden" in the camp and escaped the transport and destruction. Of this transport only 60 men survived the massacre staged by the SS guards on the road south of Munich.

On the following day, the IPC actually issued circulars informing their fellow-prisoners that the committee had taken over, that they should stay in their barracks and maintain law and order so as to prevent provocations. An attempt by the SS to evacuate another transport on the evening of 28 April failed when the inmates simply did not leave their barracks. Besides this simple aim of organizing for the purpose of saving as many lives as possible, the IPC did not have any program. There was no political activity of any kind, and no social differentiations within the group. Even the national distinction which excluded the Germans (except for Mueller) was not actively directed against the German inmates of the camp, but rather a protective measure to guard against possible sabotage of their efforts by German prisoners who were at the service of the SS. Thus even the activities of the one well-organized group emerging in the camp proved that the only rationale for organising any group activity under the conditions of Dachau was derived entirely from the primitive motive of personal survival, and not from any social, political, or religious associations.

The IPC is now the highest prisoner authority in the camp. At present it is headed by a former Soviet General (Michailow); the Belgian Haulot is Vice-President.[6] The committee has daily meetings with the army authorities and is charged with carrying out the orders issued by the American camp commandant. Sub-committees for all basic necessities, police, food, sanitation, work, disciplinary measures, etc., have been established. In this way the Committee and its various branches continues to assist in the process of maintaining order in the camp and preparing the conditions for the release and repatriation of the prisoners at Dachau.

Editor: This report was prepared by the OSS Section, Seventh Army. Its original title was "Dachau Concentration Camp."

---

6. Editor: A table prepared by the Seventh Army's CIC (see Appendix C) gives Patrick O'Leary as the President and both Nickolai Michailow and Arthur Haulot as Vice-Presidents.

2

The Camp and the Town

The very few [in the town of Dachau] who dared show some opposition ran great risk and should be honored as the courageous men and women they are. It should be pointed out, however, in justice to the others, that they were (so far as this investigation could determine) people who could seclude themselves from the community without harming their source of income.

Introduction

There are no words in English which can adequately describe the *Konzentrations-Lager* at Dachau.

In spite of the fact that one had known of its existence for years, has even spoken to people who had spent some time there, the first impression comes as a complete, a stunning shock. One had always had—in the back of one's mind—the reservation "But surely it is impossible for human beings to do this to other people."

The first thing that was seen outside of the Camp was a train of some forty railway cars of all types—mostly flat cars, a few box cars and two or three ancient third-class railway carriages. In each of the cars horribly thin corpses were lying in all postures, each clad in the [pajama] pyjama-like uniform of the concentration camps. They lay in their own refuse. Some corpses lay on the gravel road-bed, exactly where they fell when they were ordered out of the cars. There were two or three by almost every car door or gate. These were the few who were left alive when this weird train with its ghastly cargo arrived outside the gate to the camp in the afternoon of the 28 April; for these unfortunates were alive when they were loaded on. They were expected to be dead by the time they reached Dachau, so that their corpses could be done away with in the famous crematory

On the spur going directly into the Camp was another train that had recently been unloaded. Human refuse was still caked on the floors of the boxcars that had been the death chambers of unknown human beings.

American troops had arrived before the unloading of the train on the main line had been completed. At this writing proof positive of one of the greatest crimes against humanity still lies in the rickety cars and along the road bed leading into the Camp at Dachau. It lies in the shape of the broken, starved-out corpses of what once had been strong men. Men consigned to a horrible death with a cynicism brutal beyond words or belief.

The purpose of this investigation was to find out two things: (1) What conditions in the Camp actually had been like, and (2) How much did the townspeople of Dachau know of the goings-on and what was their present attitude toward this monumental crime of twelve years' duration that had transformed their sleepy little town into a world-famous place.

A total of some twenty prisoners were interviewed in the compound itself in order to determine what conditions had been like in the judgement of these men. Care was used to pick only those with red triangles on their uniforms. (This designates the political prisoner, it was found. There are also hardened criminals in the Camp, "*Schwehrverbrecher*.")

After spending the afternoon interviewing these men, the next day was spent visiting townspeople. As many parts of the town of Dachau as was possible were covered, and all possible leads were followed in order to reach as many different types of people as could be found.

While it would be fatuous to claim too much for the

results of a sampling technique such as was used in trying to get at the townspeople of Dachau, it is felt that the major types were reached, and that the dominant attitudes were discovered.

The Camp

It is extremely doubtful if one could, in any other given spot on this continent, find in two minutes' time fifteen to twenty man who would be prepared to converse with one in any of the following languages: English, French, German. Perhaps in another concentration camp.

The objectivity of these men in discussing problems was nothing short of amazing. After eight, ten and twelve years of being subjected to organized brutality, one still finds men explaining "*Ja, sehen Sie; Das ist was man muss unter einemfasis-chtischen Staat erwarten.*" ("Yes, but you see; That is what one must expect under a Fascist state"—Richard Titze.) It can be said that among the political prisoners in Dachau there is nothing that could be called a hatred of the German people as such. Their respect for anyone wearing an American uniform is deep.

These, then, are the men who gave the facts detailed below, which give a picture of what life was like in the unearthly place called *Konzentrations-Lager* Dachau.

"*Es gibt einen Weg zur Freiheit.*" ["There is a road to freedom."] Thus begins the arrogant slogan that faced these unfortunates every morning as they stood roll-call. Roll call? They were counted. From all over the compound the large white letters painted on one of the buildings can be seen. They seem to follow one around. "*Es gibt einen Weg zur Freiheit. Seine Meilensteine heissem: Gehorsem, Sauberkeit, Nuschternheit, Fleiss.*" ("There is a road to freedom. Its milestones are: Obedience, Cleanliness, Sobriety, Industry.")

Within sight of this slogan between 13,000 and 15,000 men died in the last three months alone.[1] They died mainly of starvation and of an epidemic of typhus fever. No one was

---

1. Editor: For more precise figures on deaths, see Appendix D.

concerned about the dead as far as name, family and origin were concerned. "It was merely an administrative problem involving so many corpses on such and such a morning and for which a certain number of men had to be detailed. A report was always made—stating how many carts had been used and how many corpses delivered to the crematory" (Robert Rollin). During the epidemic the crematory became overtaxed (the corpses are still piled eight feet high, stacked neatly), so that the prisoners were set to digging huge pits for mass graves. This had been done once before according to the older inhabitants. While digging the pits in which their comrades—perhaps they themselves—were to be buried, the prisoners may have thought of another ironic slogan which they saw on the grilled gate as they came in: *Arbeit Macht Frei.* ("Work Makes one Free.")

The medical care at Dachau was scarcely of the best. The director and chief surgeon of the hospital was a carpenter by trade. He performed operations personally.

"The SS rarely murdered anyone." This statement was made by Albert Kervyn, who had been an instructor in Economics at the University of Louvain. It is a bitter commentary, but it must be said to his honor and credit that he is still serving the academic ideals of objectivity and truth. He went on to explain the manner in which the Camp had been run.

The SS men, it seems, had little actual contact with the inmates. The dirty work was done by hardened criminals (*"Schwerverbrecher"*) —men who were safe-crackers by profession or who, for a small consideration, would murder a person or torture him in a pre-determined manner and think nothing of it.

This high type of human was quite often put in charge of a room, a block or group of blocks. The last *"Lagereltester"* (Camp Leader), was an Armenian who was a murderer by profession.[2] He was responsible directly to the SS *Verwaltungastab*. His men were in turn responsible to him in a well-organized hierarchy.

These were the creatures, then, who had power of life and death over teachers, lawyers, university professors, doctors, clergymen (all creeds) and assorted patriots representing practically every country in Europe. Ministers of state have spent time at Dachau.

"The SS rarely murdered anyone." But scenes in which an SS guard figured in a detached sort of way were not uncommon. According to Friedrich Mellwig, a guard might appear in a block at night, the thug in charge would yell attention (if one weren't quick about it one might be beaten on the spot). In the hearing of all the inmates a little conversation might take place: *"Wie viel Personen haben Sie hier Haute?"* *"Achtzig, Herr Unterscharfuhrer"* *"Schon gut!"* (Looks at wristwatch) *"Also—Morgenfrah ich mechte hier nur sechzing sehen."* *"Jawohl,*

---

2. Editor: The Armenian Melzarian was the next to last to hold this office (p. 23).

Herr Unterscharffuhrer!" ("How many persons have you got here today?" "Eighty, Sir!" "Very well! Now then, tomorrow morning I should like to see only sixty here." "Very well Sir!") That night a detail of twenty men would be told off.

"The SS rarely murdered anyone, but you can bully a man to death, you know—particularly if he is old, was once proud, and you have cut down his rations to three potatoes a day," to conclude Kervyn's statement.

The manner of dying at Dachau was as varied as it was unpleasantly gruesome. It is sickening to detail them.

A detail might be told off to disappear into the crematory, never to be seen again. It was most unwise to ask questions.

A man's rations—or those of a whole block—might be systematically cut down. The most horrible sight at Dachau is the corpses who are still actually alive.

A detail might be told off on a cold winter's night, marched off into an unfrequented place in the huge compound, told to strip until naked, and then have a hydrant turned on them. In the morning a cart (manned by another detail) would collect the corpses.

A men [man] might become "insubordinate"—i.e., he might cry "Stop!" while being beaten. In such a case he was taken to the room where other "dangerous" characters were trussed up, wrists behind back, feet just above the floor, was tied in a similar manner—and left there.

Over the long and infamous history of this place, the most common way of dying was "on transport." Hence the crematory. Random examples: From a transport of 200 Belgians in last July, 70 dead; transport of French civilians arrived last October consisting of eight flat cars in which there were 484 dead on arrival. The few who could walk away were beaten to death on the spot by the guards. Asked by the interviewer whether this were not an unusual instance, Adolf Weber laughed and said: *"Hier hatten Sie beinahe jeden Tag so ein Bild sehch konnen!"* ("You could have seen such a spectacle here almost every day!")

The Townspeople

It seems possible to define three broad groups among the Dachau populace with respect to their attitudes toward the grisly death camp on the edge of their town. The worst, of course, have left (the SS officials and their families). This is a fact that was confirmed both by inmates of the Camp and the townspeople. An interesting side-light on the preparations for evacuation made long in advance by these characters is furnished by the incident reported by a Fraulein Scherrer. Some time ago she was walking down a street behind the wife of an SS Hauptstrumfuhrer. As a work-detail of inmates passed by in the striped uniforms, the little child of the SS man tattled, "Mama, Papa has a striped suit just like those at home too!" The woman glanced around and said to the child, "Don't you ever say such a thing again!"

"Wir sind aberall belogen worden." ["We have all been lied to."] These words crop up again and again. It is the rationalization of the man who admits, like Franz Egger, that he was a member of the Nazi Party. They generally add a hasty, "I was forced to by business reasons." This type invariably claims that, "We were lied to in every respect." They admit that they knew the Camp existed, that they saw work-details of inmates passing through the streets under guard, that "in

some instances" (particularly in the years of 34 and 35) the SS behaved brutally—toward the townspeople.

When asked whether they realize that in the last three months a minimum of 13,000 man have lost their lives within a stone's throw of where they live, they claim shocked surprise.

When asked whether they ever saw transports of dead and dying pass through the streets along the railway, they refer only to the last one. They insist that most of the trains came in at night, and that they were sealed cars. Did they never ask what was in the endless procession of cars that came in full and always went out empty? *"Es ist uns erzahlt worden, dass das wur Wehrmachtsmaterial und Beutomaterial aus Frankreich."* ("We were told that it was all Army material and booty from France"—Egger.) It can definitely be stated that anyone in Dachau who now claims to have seen only one train of prospective inmates come in the day time is telling a flat lie. There are quite a few such people in Dachau.

"Was konnten wir tun?" ["What could we have done?"] This statement would seem to represent the most popular attitude in the town of Dachau at present. Josef Scherrer is a typical example of this attitude. Here is a man who was without doubt an anti-Nazi. He had come into conflict with the authorities on numerous occasions because of his anti-Nazi attitude, and the Lendrat [*Landrat*] had already issued a warrant for his arrest by the SS. He was saved in the last minute by his physician who was a good friend of the *Landrat*—also he might very well have been one of the people on the inside of the compound.

The picture given by this man of what life was like in Dachau for people of human decency and some conscience is not a pleasant one.

Scherrer insists that the people of Dachau knew very well

what was going on in the Camp. He states that resentment was fairly general, particularly because the SS misbehaved toward the civilian population as well. He says that this aspect was at its worst in the years 33, 34 and 35. Civilians quite often tried to give food to inmates who were on work details, but were almost invariably prevented from so doing by the SS guards. In the last year the SS guards became more lenient in this respect, since large numbers of them had been drafted into the SS against their will. (This is a well-known fact which was discovered some time ago in P/W [prisoner-of-war] interrogations. Several inmates also told the story of how, in last October, a whole SS Regiment was recruited—from of all sources, the inmates of Dachau Concentration Camp. These men were all *Reichsdeutsche* and under 40 years old. They were given no choice. *"Das war reiner Zwang."* ("That was pure force"—Weber.) Inmates of all nationalities also admitted that recently the townspeople had been better toward them in the matter of giving them food when they were out on work details).

Although the population as a whole realized the utter bestiality of the SS and the nauseating occurrences beyond the barred gates of the Camp, they were afraid even to say anything—much less do something—because the shadow of the Camp hung over them as well. Several persons claimed that such cases had actually happened, and that people were even afraid to watch prisoner transports being brought in for fear that they themselves might be interned for the mere knowledge of the crimes. The whole system was obviously based on the barbaric theory that, "Dead men tell no tales."

These people admit that the town as a whole did a thriving business as a result of the presence of the Camp and its attendant SS *"Bonzen"* ("Big Shots") —and it is perhaps not without significance that the most outspoken anti-Nazis were people who, so to speak, could afford to be so by reason of the fact that their business did not bring them into daily contact with the SS.

"Es war alles sehr entzetzlich, aber was konnten wir tun?" ("It was all very horrible, but what could we do?"—Martin Witt-

mann.)

"Ein Schandfleck fur die ganze zivilisierte Menachheit!" ("A scandal for all of civilized humanity!") With these words of the outraged Herr Josef Engelhard the attitude of those few people in Dachau who dared to protest—more or less openly—for all these years is comprehended.

When asked in how far he considered his fellow-townsmen responsible for what went on in the Camp, he replied: *"Neunzig prozent sind schmutzig und haben sich mit dem Blut unschuldiger Menschen bes udelt!"* ("Ninety per cent are dirty and have daubed themselves with the blood of innocent human beings!")

Engelhard lives on the street (called the Nibelungen Strasse, incidentally) along which the cars rolled to the Camp. His house is situated only a few hundred yards from the entrance to that Charnel-house. He corroborated the stories of the inmates about the fearful cargoes that had been brought in through the years. They began to be really horrible after 1938. The huge transports of Jews at that time were "too horrible to describe." Shortly after the invasion "thousands upon thousands of Frenchmen" were brought in. One such transport of French stopped directly in front of his house. When the doors of the boxcars were opened, most of the dead were beginning to decay. After the collapse of the Warsaw uprising, transports of Poles began to arrive in great numbers and in indescribable states. The few who were alive in one such load scrambled out of the cars and—it was evident from his expression that Herr Engelhard still had difficulty in believing what his own eyes had seen—*"Die haben Gras gefressen und aus Pfatzen getrunken!"* ("They ate grass and drank out of puddles!")

The old Social Democrat and president of his trade union, who had never once raised his hand in a Nazi salute (this was confirmed by other people), said he was very much against executing Nazis. *"Das ist zu gut fur dies Bande."* ("That is too good for this gang.") He suggests sending them to Siberia in transports "exactly like those that have been arriving daily in Dachau for years." He added that he had no doubt that, "Herr Stalin  has much room for them and much for them to do." He concluded by saying, *"Endlich mus die ganze Nazi-Brut ausgerotten werden!"* ("Finally the entire Nazi-Spawn must be exterminated!")

In the opinion of this minority, the people are to blame for their cowardice. Old, gracious and intelligent Eduard Grasal feels very strongly on this point. He has a right to talk. He was one of three men in the entire town who stood up in open meeting and said he would not join the Storm Troops, "Because, my dear Major, I won't!"—and with this he walked out of the meeting. Weeks later dozens of people came to him and said, "But if we had only known that they wouldn't do anything to us, we would have stood up too!" He cites this as an example: *"Feig und Feiglinge! Die waren alle zu feig—Die wollten uberhaupt nichts riskieren. Und es war so in ganz Deutschland. Die mutige sind en den Handen abzuzahlen."* ("Cowardly and cowards! They were all too cowardly—They really didn't want to risk anything. And that's the way it was in all Germany. The courageous can be counted on the fingers of your hands.")

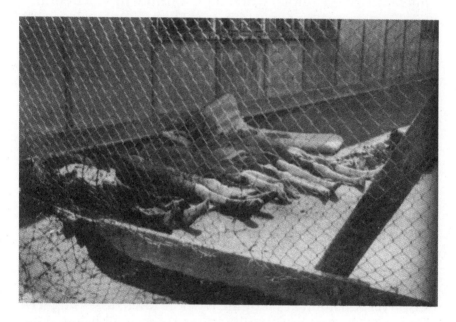

Conclusion

No citizen of Dachau is without a deep sense that something was wrong, terribly wrong, on the outskirts of their town.

The majority of them take the position described above. That they are honest in this attitude for the most part allows of no doubt whatever.

Those who didn't give a tinker's damn what happened to the poor souls whom they saw pass through their streets for years—so long as business was good and the SS Hauptsturmfuhrer paid his handsome rent—were really few. Today they are the ones who plead *"Ja—wir wussten uberhaupt nichts was passiert da draussent!"* ("But we really didn't know what was going on out there!") *"Da draussen"*—as if it were on another planet! They are liars, and guilty as sin—every one.

The very few who dared show some opposition ran great risk and should be honored as the courageous men and women they are. It should be pointed out, however, in justice to the others, that they were (so far as this investigation could determine) people who could seclude themselves from the community without harming their source of income. Herr Engelhard, for example, worked for a firm which sent him travelling over all Southern Europe. Herr Grasal had a small importing business from Italy. They could both afford to isolate themselves (as they did) in their houses for years. Herr Grasal—who is obviously the type who likes his *Gemutlichkeit*—said that he had never gone into a tavern for years for fear he "might talk too freely." He gave up all entertaining at his home seven years ago. By contrast Herr Scherrer, who was not so extreme in his remarks, emerges as a man who has suffered far more and who had every bit as much courage. He made his living by running a restaurant. For a known anti-Nazi in a town which was a Nazi *"Hochburg"* and a cradle of the SS this is no small achievement. *"Meine Nerven sind vollkommen zur Grunde gegangen"* ("My nerves are totally shot"), he says. Small wonder.

If one is to attempt the tremendous task and accept the terrific responsibility of judging a whole town, assessing it *en masse* as to the collective guilt or innocence of all its inhabitants for this most hideous of crimes, one would do well to remember the fearsome shadow that hangs over everyone in a state in which crime has been incorporated and called the government.

Editor: This report was prepared by the PWB Section, U.S. Seventh Army. Its original title was "Dachau Concentration Camp and Town."

3

Life and Death at Dachau

Sunday, just after the noon meal, the air was unusually still. The big field outside the compound was deserted. Suddenly someone began running toward the gate at the other side of the field. Others followed. The word was shouted through the mass of gray, tired prisoners. Americans! That word repeated, yelled over the shoulders in throaty Polish, in Italian, in Russian, and Dutch and in the familiar ring of French.

Memorandum

On 29 April 1945, the liberation of the Dachau Concentration Camp, Dachau, Germany, presented to the Allied Armies a gruesome spectacle of wholesale bestiality and barbarism. A section of the Counter Intelligence Corps Detachment, Seventh Army, was dispatched to the camp for counter intelligence work, and was requested to submit a report of general interest on the camp as documentary evidence for higher headquarters.

The notorious Dachau Concentration Camp, the first to be organized by the Nazi Regime, is located 18 kilometers northwest of Munich, Germany. Up to 1933, it was used[1] solely for confinement of political prisoners, and in addition, men who were released from other German prisons were often confined here for 'Protective Custody,' after completing their sentences. In 1936, when the Nazis were organizing for world conquest, people who did not cooperate with the program were interned here. Well over 229,000 internees have

---

1. Editor: Since the camp opened on March 22, 1933, this should probably read, "Up to 1936, it was used . . ."

passed through Dachau since 1933.

Before the war, the number of internees varied from 6,000 to 8,000.[2] There were Jews in Dachau in 1933, but the first outstanding numbers began to arrive in 1936. In 1939, owing to international affairs, some Jews were released and allowed to emigrate, but after hostilities began, their numbers vastly increased in Dachau.

When the American troops arrived on 29 April 1945, there were approximately 32,500 estimated internees of all nationalities, the Poles predominating. During this period, the camp was notorious for its cruelty, but within the last six or eight months, some "token" improvement was noted in the treatment of the internees. However, the new crematorium was completed in May 1944, and the gas chambers, a total of five, were used for the executions and the disposals of the bodies.

Three weeks prior to the arrival of American troops, the more important records, papers, card index systems, etc., were burned or otherwise removed.

In addition of [to] the Dachau Camp, there were 21 subsidiary camps, all under the jurisdiction of the Dachau Administration.

Liberation

The Americans came Sunday, 29th of April. The arrival of the Americans was preceded by several days of frenzy. Wednesday was the last day of work, and there was no more going out of the compound. Scattered labor details living outside of camp returned suddenly. Radios were taken away and there was no more communication with the outside.

On Thursday, orders to evacuate the entire camp were given. Transports began to be organized on large scales, but the organization was poor and uncoordinated. The prisoners having jobs in the administrative department mislaid orders, suddenly did not understand commands, and generally seemed quite indifferent to the mounting nervousness of the

2. Editor: For approximate figures for different periods, see Appendix D.

few camp officials that were left. Only one transport got under way. It consisted of about 4,000 men, and they hiked with heavy guard in the direction of the Tyrol.

Then began the time of tense waiting. Rumors swept through the barracks of regiments and tanks just over the hill, of plans of mass annihilation of the prisoners by the remaining SS men, of parachutists, and of an armistice. The prisoners organized a secret police force to keep order after the liberation they knew was coming. They built barricades to keep their own comrades from getting in the way of the jumpy guards. And all time was at a standstill for three days while the prisoners waited and the guards paced nervously, furtively, in their towers.

Sunday, just after the noon meal, the air was unusually still. The big field outside the compound was deserted. Suddenly someone began running toward the gate at the other side of the field. Others followed. The word was shouted through the mass of gray, tired prisoners. Americans! That word repeated, yelled over the shoulders in throaty Polish, in Italian, in Russian, and Dutch and in the familiar ring of French. The first internee was shot down as he rushed toward the gate by the guard. Yet they kept running and shouting through eager lips and unbelieving eyes. Americans! And at the gate in front of the hysterical mob of men were not the regiments or the tanks they had expected, but one dark-complexioned, calm American soldier, an American Pole, pistol in hand, looking casually about him; up at the towers where the SS guards watched apparently frozen; behind him two or three other American boys about a hundred yards away; and into the flushed wet faces of those thousands surging about in front of him.

A few shots were fired from behind the wall, the guards in the first tower came down, hands above their heads. A white blanket was hung out from another tower, and they came down, but one of them had a pistol in his hand which he held behind his back, and the dark-complexioned soldier shot him down. At the far side of the compound, the guards were taken care of from the outside.

Then a jeep arrived. Where were the regiments and tanks? The first American was hoisted into the air and two others, a 19-year-old farmer from the West, and a 19-year-old university student, were dragged out of the jeep and carried around the grounds on the internees' shoulders. A blond journalist in uniform[3] was also in the jeep, and she climbed the tower by the gate with a young officer.

Suddenly the prisoners produced flags and colors which had been buried under barracks or hidden in rafters. These

3. Editor: This was apparently Marguerite "Maggie" Higgins, a well-known reporter for the *New York Herald Tribune*. For further details see *Dachau, 29 April 1945*. Her 1955 autobiography is *News is a Singular Thing*.

flags and colors were improvised from sheets and scraps of colored cloth. It was a mardi-gras. Over the loud speaker system the blond journalist said, "We are just as glad to see you as you are to see us." And then a chaplain in broken German asked them to join him in the Lord's Prayer. And for a few minutes in powerful earnest unison and with bowed reverent heads and clasped hands, they prayed. The words echoed through the compound and through the hearts of the thousands still incredulous at the dark-complexioned American Pole, the 19-year-old farm boy from the West, and the student, and at the regiments and tanks that never came.

Life at Dachau

Reception of Internees

Internees arriving at Dachau were processed, screened, and segregated according to nations. Internees were transported like cattle to Dachau. One witness relates his journey from France. He was herded into a boxcar with 98 men. Three of them survived the slow, endless journey, and the other two died within a few days. During the screening, internees were beaten up and tortured in order to get certain information which the *Politische Abteilung* (Political Department) felt was being held back. They were assembled again, and placed into quarantine barracks, where they remained for 21 days. After the 21 days, they were assigned to their permanent barracks (*blocks*) in Dachau or its subsidiary camps.

Daily Routine

The internees were gotten up at 5:30 in the winter, and at 4:00 in the summer. After washing, they all received a cup of black coffee, nothing else. Then they fell out according to barracks, and were marched over to the assembly area where interminable roll call was taken. After this, the work commander would call out the various work details for the day, and the internees would reassemble according to their respective work groups. Everyone of those placed on the work detail was given a slice of bread about one-quarter inch thick and a slice of sausage which had to last until noon. At 11:30, they marched back into the camp, and back to their barracks, where they received their dinner, which consisted of small portion of cabbage, carrots, and sometimes potatoes. At 12:30, they marched out to work again, and worked until 6 o'clock, and then back to camp. The evening *appell* (roll call) was taken, and then the men returned to their barracks for supper. The supper consisted of, three times a week, a little soup, and an eighth of bread; and two days a week, they received a slice of bread, and either a slice of sausage or a bit of cheese.

The numerous work details comprised upkeep of grounds and buildings, construction work details, outfitting works for uniforms for SS men, the paper factory in Dachau, the porcelain works in Allach, the small arms factory in the camp proper, and the *Plantage*—the farm land near the camp. It is estimated that approximately 3,000 Jews died on the *Plantages*. When the camp officials felt that these internees were too ill and too weak to work, they would march them into a lake (since drained), regardless of the time of year. They were forced to stay in the water until dead. Those who remained conscious were placed in wheelbarrows, brought back to camp, where they died a few hours later.

The Kiesgrube detail was considered the worst work detail the internees could be put on. They would have to load wagons with crushed rock at a speed which caused the internees to collapse and die on the spot.

Experimental Stations

SS Ahnenerbe[4]

Jews were selected for this experiment. A truck, completely equipped, would roll up to between Barracks 3 and 5. The internee selected for this experiment was placed in a cylinder, and the air pressure lowered to a point which coincided with air pressure at an altitude of 5,000 to 8,000 meters. The air pressure was then brought back to normal sea level pressure at a terrific speed. These conditions simulated a parachutist dropping at a terrific speed, much greater than can be encountered in reality. The reactions of men undergoing these experiments were observed and studied for future air force training. Not a single man was seen leaving this truck alive.[5]

The Water Tank—Exposure Experiments

There was a water tank about 12 feet deep, filled with cold water, temperature of which was 1 degrees Centigrade. Internees were forced to dive in and stay in at various lengths of time, until unconscious.[6] Then they were placed in bed with female internees brought over from Ravensbruck Concentration Camp solely for this experiment, evidently to test the effectiveness of body temperature.[7]

---

4. Editor: *Ahnenerbe*, which literally means "ancestral heritage," was a SS research institute. It tried to prove Nazi doctrines about the superiority of the Aryan race and was under the direct control of Heinrich Himmler.
5. Editor: Those wanting to know more about the high altitude experiments can consult: Alexander Mitscherlich, *Doctors of Infamy* (Henry Schuman: New York, 1949), 4–19. Some 70 to 80 inmates died due to them.
6. Editor: These experiments were intended to discover how to treat aviators who came down in cold water. Some 300 inmates were used in them and about 80 to 90 died. The experiments established that rapid rewarming in hot water was more effective than placing the chilled person next to one or more naked women. For more details, see *Doctors of Infamy*, 20–33.

Blood Experimentations

A blood analysis was made of internees chosen for these experiments. Their purposes are not clear, but all victims undergoing these blood experiments went insane. The day before American troops took over the concentration camp, all persons who had undergone these experiments were shot.

The first two above (the air pressure and water tank) experiments were completed about a year ago. The last (blood experiments) were continued up to four weeks prior to American occupation.

Malaria Experimental Station

All internees chosen for the malaria experiments had to be physically and mentally fit. Nearly all Polish priests had undergone the malaria experiments. Two methods of malarial inoculation were used. The first was by means of human blood infected by malaria, and the second was by means of using infected mosquitoes and permitting them to bite the patients. The first group of experiments consisted of inoculating these individuals with malaria, permitting them to have varying numbers of chills. This was done in an attempt to determine whether or not the facilities of cure differed depending upon the number of attacks of fever. The second set of experiments consisted of inoculating healthy people with the malaria, and when the prodromal symptoms developed, to start treatment before chills and fever had occurred. The third group of experiments were conducted using a drug

---

7. Editor: A British intelligence report released 18 September 1945 noted: "Former prisoners who gave technical assistance now claim to have 'cooked' results for humane reasons. Thus a worker dealing with laboratory specimens produced reports ostensibly confirming earlier findings, hoping thereby to prevent further sacrifice of internees for corroborative experiments; and a man who recorded rectal temperatures claims to have adjusted the galvanometer to give unduly low readings so that victims might be removed earlier from the bath." C. C. Ungley, *Research and Development of Life Saving Equipment, Medical Aspects of Shipwreck, Report on Visit to Occupied Europe, July 1945.* British Intelligence Objectives Sub-Committee. B.I.O.S Final Report No. 494, Item No. 24. p. 57.

known as "Pyramidon" which suppressed the fever in malaria, but did not cure the disease.

Phlegmone

These experiments were begun in 1942, and were carried out in Block 1 B. Six Jews were injected with germs and died. Another group of ten internees were injected intermuscularly [intramuscularly] in the legs and contracted phlegmonia. Then they received new injections in the other leg, and those who still remained alive received new injections in the arm. None of this group survived.[8]

In October 1942, further experiments were carried out. Twenty prisoners were selected from Block 20. They received intermuscular [intramuscular] injections of pus. Some of these were treated by bio-chemical pills, eight with sulfonamid, four were treated for wounds. Six died.

Subsequently, a group of 40 priests were subjected to these experiments. Half of them were treated bio-chemically, the other half with sulfonamid, but all prophylactically. In the first group, nine died from resultant complications.

One intern admits that a large group of patients with severe cases of phlegmone was treated with bio-chemical pills, without being operated on, until the wounds opened, or the patient died. Bio-chemical pills were used for different kinds of diseases such as ascites, pneumonia, and others.

All patients undergoing these experiments were photographed each week or every two weeks. According to the male intern, these experiments were ordered by the Reich's leaders and controlled by someone from Munich.

The total number of victims of these experiments is estimated to be 300. About 56 died during the experiments, about 30 from complications.

The chief surgeon read a letter from Himmler in which it was stated that these researches by the doctors were obvi-

---

8. Editor: These seem to be the cellulitis experiments described in *Doctors of Infamy* (p. 66-75). One witness testified that 19 men died in them.

ously being sabotaged by them. The doctors conducting these experiments were of the opinion that these researches were of unscientific nature.

Executions

Gas Chambers

The internees who were brought to Camp Dachau for the sole purpose of being executed were in most cases Jews and Russians. They were brought into the compound, lined up near the gas chambers, and were screened in a  similar manner as internees who came to Dachau for imprisonment. Then they were marched to a room and told to undress. Everyone was given a towel and a piece of soap, as though they were about to take a shower. During this whole screening process, no hint was ever given that they were to be executed, for the routine was similar upon the arrival of all internees at the camp.

Then they entered the gas chamber, Over the entrance, in large black letters, was written *"Brause Bad"* (showers). There were about 15 shower faucets suspended from the ceiling from which gas was then released. There was one large chamber, capacity of which was 200, and five smaller gas chambers, capacity of each being 50. It took approximately 10 minutes for the execution. From the gas chamber, the door led to the *Krematory* to which the bodies were removed by internees who were selected for the job. The dead bodies were then placed in five furnaces, two to three bodies at a time.

Krematorium

The *Krematorium* was operated by SS personnel of the *Abteilung-I-Kommandatur* (Personal Staff Section) with the help of seven to ten specially chosen internees. These were usually Jews who were taken out of their barracks, and lodged in the so-called "dungeon." They were well-fed and well-treated, but had to work all day long in the *Krematory*.

After five or six weeks, when their knowledge of key personnel was such that they became dangerous, they were executed and several more Jews were chosen to take up their functions.

Gun Executions

Most of the gun executions were used on Russian officers and soldiers. The non-commissioned officer in charge of the *block* (barracks) would call out the names, the selected internees would fall out and would be marched to the gate which separates the internee compound and the administrative sections of the camp. Here the SS men who volunteered for the execution squad would lead them out to the *"Schiesstand"* (shooting stand) near the *Krematory*, had the victims kneel down, lower their heads. and were shot in back of their necks. Eight to ten men at a time were executed in that manner. In September 1944, ninety-one Russian officers were executed in one day.

This photograph of the "Schiesstand" is one of the most unimpressive pictorially, but the blood-soaked ground, the smell and feeling of death make this spot one of the most ghastly in Dachau.

Editor: This report was prepared by the CIC Detachment. Seventh Army. Its original name was "Dachau, Concentration Camp." The report continues in the next two chapters and the appendices.

4

The Diary of E. K.

> I was talking to a friend today. Some months ago he left with a transport to Mauthausen. There were 1600 of them. Now after nine months, he too returned, as in another world. More dead than alive, he was . . . he and the remaining nineteen men. That means that 20 men remained out of 1600. Yes, Dachau is, in spite of everything, the golden camp.

One of the most interesting documents unearthed by this section of the CIC Detachment was a water-logged diary kept from November 1942 until recent days. This diary was written by E.K., internee since 1940. In secret and under the greatest difficulties, E.K. was able to record the events of the days. Discovery meant certain death. The incidents and situations described were personal experiences of E.K. and of his closest friends. The diary, written in German, is much too long to be incorporated in whole in this report. Excerpts are submitted as an illustration of the tone of the whole and as attestation to the acts of barbarism committed in the Dachau Concentration Camp. Both the author and his work may be in danger of German reprisals.[1]

20 November 1942

These pages that I now begin to write would lead to certain death if ever they were found. But what is death? How few of

---

1. Editor: The writer was Edgar Kupfer-Koberwitz, later the author of *Tierbrüder* (1947), *Die Mächtigen und die Hilflosen* (1957), and *Dachauer Tagebücher* (1997). Unfortunately, other than this brief but moving excerpt, none of his writings seem have been translated into English.

those I know here are still alive today, how close to death we all stand! I can die here any moment, even if I take the greatest care.

Why should I not endeavor, even in the midst of these conditions, of this cruelty, to tell this gruesome story that no longer gives us goose flesh?

I feel, I know not why, the urge to write.

I really thought I would record all this for you, so that when we will meet again some time later, I would have nothing more to say; I would give you the pages and be silent—for I am tired of speaking.

And now I hasten to begin, without regarding the danger it involves. My friends think I am secretly writing a poem, most likely a love poem, or one about flowers and stars. If they knew what I was doing, they would burn these pages out of fear. In fact, they would be right, because I endanger their lives as well as my own; only they don't know it. And if these lines were found, I should have to prove that they had no knowledge of my secret writing, for I only showed them harmless little verses.

21 November 1942.

Something happened yesterday that excited even the most hardened of us, and that means something, for we have lost all feeling, nothing more can astonish us in any way. And so it was yesterday. Very few of us were moved, just those who were directly concerned.

Five hundred invalids came yesterday from a camp near Danzig. To be an invalid among us prisoners means to be at death's door. Later, when we are together, I will tell you more about that.

Fifty-one of these "invalids" came in dead, but their bodies had already been partly eaten by the others, the remains and bones were thrown out of the chink in the cattle-truck door during the journey. Only a few unrecognizable parts of the body remained. The whole side was missing from one body, from others the nose, or cheek, or genital organs.

It must have been a terrible sight; I am so thankful I did not see it.

All the corpses were photographed. Most likely the camp authorities did this to send evidence to Berlin. The prisoners, during the six days that their journey lasted, received only one piece of bread, six hundred grams, I believe. Hunger delirium broke out among them, as they had suffered for a long time from under feeding. The officers of our guard, who otherwise make fun and joke about all these horrible things, except those concerning them, were moved. This time they had seen something new: cannibalism, and that they were not used to. The last remains of civilization surged against these facts and deeds.

Forty-nine of the survivors died yesterday, the day of their arrival. Soon there will be more and every day the number will increase. That they brought them here can only be explained by the fact that manpower is needed; so they move up all they can. Of those that can't be revived . . . of those, I will speak to you later. Will you ever read these pages? Each page is a source of danger and who knows how many pages I will write, but even if I can put down all I experience . . . it is so hard to hide these pages. May a good power protect them and keep them in safety, so that one day I can give them to you, together with a heart of stone that was wrought for you secretly during days and days and that I wore for a long time. Perhaps these pages will survive me, and some stranger will bring them to you.

The most beautiful flowers on my tomb, the tomb of my remembrance, for who dies here has no material grave.

I have grown older. My temples are turning grey and age is changing my features. I sometimes notice it when I look at myself in the small mirror of the washroom. I am only 36 years old, but, as most of us, my hair turning grey . . . "silver threads among the gold," as in the song.

22 November 1942.

I must tell you something that shocked me so much today; I don't know myself why.

It is Sunday. We are standing on the roll call court and are waiting for the order to march out. Beside us a few hundred Russians, or rather Ukrainians are led up. The two first lines are . . . children of 11 to 15. Their small bodies clad in garments far too large for them; their pale faces with childish, half joyful eyes, their voices sound like the lark's song in a church yard.

Last Sunday someone led past me a dying, whimpering infant. I had to turn my face away . . . help here is quite impossible.

These children, these young fellows worked in Wurtenburg, near Ulm. Food there was so scarce that they starved, They escaped in groups . . . they wanted to return home. Instead of that they were sent here. Many of them are already dead. They are quite happy about here . . . they say that food here is better. They are quite happy about that, and that tells its own tale. Hearts must grow hard here, otherwise one would cry from morn till evening.

8 December 1942.

Today is already December the 8th. Nothing happens, only small, trivial things.

At night, in bed I drew the blankets over my head, but I heard what somebody was saying behind us. His friend is a litter bearer . . . the job doesn't move him any longer. Yesterday as he was piling up the corpses, his attention was accidentally drawn to one face . . . it was his brother.

How he must have been shocked, although he was used to handling corpses. His brother had come from another camp without his knowing it.

Someone came and pulled the blankets from my head. It was a Polish friend of mine. He told me about a priest, a schoolmate of his. Here in Dachau they met again. The priest was suddenly taken into the *Revier*—that is the name they give to the hospital here, to be experimented on. Research is being made here on boils.[2]

Twenty-six priests of Polish and Czech origin died from these experiments. In spite of this, the work went on just as the one on malaria.

The priest secretly sent a short note to his friend. The last sentence was not legible, for, as he himself said, he had 40 degree temperature. He did not ask for help because he knew all was lost. He only prayed that a way be found to prepare his family for the worst. He will be operated on Friday.

---

2. Editor: During the war, the Nazis sent 3,646 Polish priests to concentration camps and out of that number 2,647 (73%) died. Among Polish nuns, 1,117 were imprisoned with 238 of those executed and 25 dying of other causes (a death toll of 24%). At various times, 1,474 Polish priests were kept at Dachau and some 120 were killed in various medical experiments there and elsewhere. See George Weigel, *Witness to Hope* (New York: Harper Collins, 1999), 52.

The prisoners are inoculated with these boils and then when the illness is at its highest point, they apply the countermeasure. They are experimenting.

Many hundreds will still die in this way and we must look on, helpless and unable to do anything. Each one must see how he can escape death, today, this very hour.

Tomorrow, tomorrow cannot be known.

And day before yesterday another 300 invalids came in. It was Sunday, and, as I was at work, I did not see them. People told me they were merely living corpses, and those who saw them thought that within two days more than half would be dead.

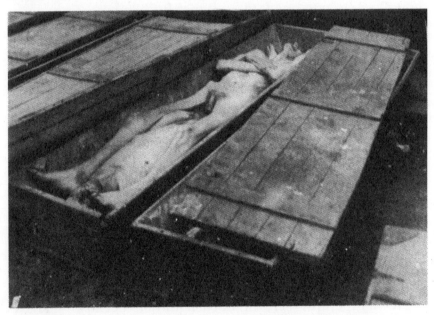

Another friend made me very sad today. His wife, whom he loves and who loved him, left his parents and her child and went to another country. He doesn't know why. Would it be to work?

He is weak and sensitive. I am surprised that he is still alive and now this happens to him.

It is like an illness. The wives outside get tired of waiting and claim divorce. Now the men don't receive their wives and children are lost to them, and with that, all ideals, all hold on life.[3]

Just now a friend who works beside me told me that his father died. He was buried with full military honors. Now the mother doesn't want to receive any more news from her son, as he bears a part of the responsibility for his father's death. What do these outside think we are . . . we here inside the camp? In fact, I know it has been spread about that only the most dangerous subjects, traitors and the like, among those the most severe cases, remain locked up here and in other camps. If only they saw us here, if only they knew. They think that a few hundred people are still interned.

But only here there are always between 8,000 and 12,000 men. In spite of the deaths, the number always remains about the same, as the Gestapo is working day and night. There are camps we have heard about that contain between 20,000 and 100,000 prisoners, men and women.

It is a real shame. In other camps so many more die. Proportionately, few die here, on an average of 10 a day. That is being very cautious, but it gives a frightening total: one man out of every three has to die within the year.

10 December 1942.

Yesterday, I saw again thin men creeping out of the front room of our barracks, They had stolen potato peelings out of the dust bin and filled their pockets with them. They were old and young men. Hunger hurts, and the majority haven't the willpower to master the gnawing of the stomach.

But, as compared to other camps, this is heaven. One of our prisoners coming from Mauthausen told me today that there they had daily from 40 to 50 casualties out of a total of 4,000 to 6,000 men. On a certain winter day, the number went up to 180.

Only those who have lived and seen all that can believe that.

---

3. Editor: Perhaps this should read, "Now the men perceive their wives and children are lost to them . . ."

17 December 1942

Actually, instead of many guards, we often only have 2 SS men, each with his Alsatian bloodhound when we march back to camp after work. How times change! Before, when we were 80 men, we had 18 guards, now we are 150. Man becomes scarce.

19 December 1942.

They say that there are three cases of typhus in the camp. If that is true, we can still expect to witness all sorts of things.

20 December 1942.

Two men died today in the camp from typhus. It is said four others caught the illness, Russians and Italians.

Those nationals are cooped up in large numbers in the

barracks and therefore have lice, the greatest agents of propagation of the illness, so that many more cases can be expected.

They are disinfecting. Can that be of any use?

Yesterday, or the day before, Sister Pia was in camp. They said she was moved by the condition of the Polish priests. In one year, 800 of about 2,000 men died. That is counting too little; 1,200 could have died. They all look like skeletons. One of the bishops also died.

Oh pity! When and how will I at last be able to tell all to you. But how can I find words to do it!

21 December 1942.

The inmates had to run nude to the baths and had to return naked. (This is in the end of December). Sanitary measures, they call it.

In addition, the camp was controlled for lice. Five-hundred men were infected by lice. All their personal belongings were disinfected: shirts, coats, blankets, everything. Does it help? Perhaps. . .

During the winter of 1941, in January, I stood naked among 500 men for one hour on the roll call court to be checked like animals, whether we were transportable to the camp of Nenegamme, whose climate and work and conditions of this camp destroyed man [men] so fast that time and again they had to get new slaves from Dachau and other camps.

22 December 1942.

One of the former block leaders is said to be hospitalized in the *Revier*. It isn't such a long time since he left for the front. We called him the "Hamburger," a giant, brutal face, only 20 years old, paws like those of a rhinoceros. Only a year ago or maybe it was this year, he beat a man to death because this man had eaten potato peelings, but he did not kill him slowly, as is customary; no, he killed him with one blow of his fist. He was too weak, the other too strong. He was also one of those who took pleasure in horse-whippings. Many have already been killed by him or have been hastened to death at the whipping place.

They say that he lost one hand and one leg.

Fate had caught up with him, if it is true. Now he cannot either beat or kick any more. I wonder if his heart has changed too.

23 December 1942.

Our hospital, the *Revier*, has been put under quarantine. The sick ward is now in the bath room. Typhus now seems to be getting serious. We went to the baths to bathe. A transport of invalids had arrived. On many of the invalids, the shoulder blades stuck out like wings. They did not walk . . . those who could keep themselves erect dragged their feet absent-mindedly.

I thought of the time when I myself returned to this camp. What a wonder that I am still alive.

I was talking to a friend today. Some years [months] ago he left with a transport to Mauthausen. There were 1600 of them. Now after nine months, he too returned, as in another world. More dead than alive, he was . . . he and the remaining nineteen men. That means that 20 men remained out of 1600. Yes, Dachau is, in spite of everything, the golden camp.

25 December 1942

Our first holiday. We had to rise naked at 7 o'clock. Naked, we had to run 250 yards to the baths, holding our eating equipment in our hands. We stayed for seven hours in the baths, naked, but the place was heated. We were disinfected. After seven hours we returned to our blocks. The irritating gas here hurt our eyes, so that we had to go outside again. The barracks had been gassed for delousing.

The entire night we were forced to sleep with windows open, but our eyes were watery, our heads ached. A curious holiday, our first Christmas day.

Today they told me about Russia. One of my friends was an eyewitness. In this town lived about 350,000 Russians, of whom 90,000 [were] Jews, They were driven out of the city, dressed only in shirts, in winter, in unbearable cold. There they had to dig graves, women, men and children. They were forced to stand in front of them. Then they were mowed down by machine guns. They were pushed into graves, living or dead, it didn't matter and were covered with earth. He said that in another village, they brought the people to a Jewish cemetery, and then when they were herded together, the cemetery was blown up. This is the news from outside world. It isn't pretty, but credible, for we know their methods.

Editor: This chapter is a continuation of the CIC report begun in Chapter 3. It was originally entitled, "Diary of E. K."

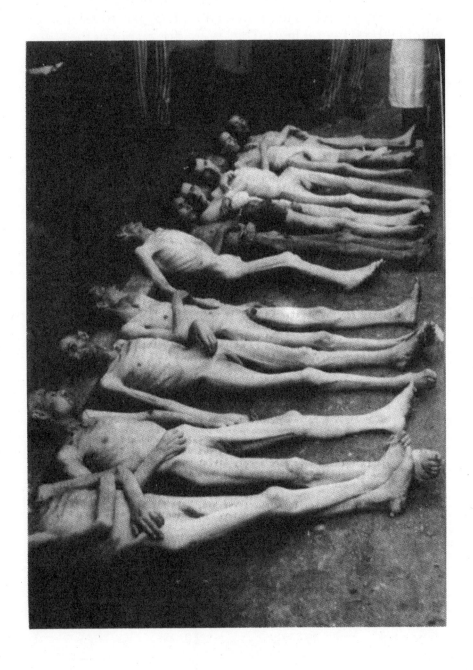

CHAPTER

5

Rudolf Hoess' Mistress

According to my recollection, on December 16, 1942, about
11 P.M. I was already asleep, suddenly the C.O. appeared
before me. I hadn't heard the opening of my cell and was
such frightened. It was dark in the cell. I believed at first it
was an SS man or a prisoner and said, "What is this tomfoolery, I forbid you." Then I heard "Pst," and a pocket
lamp was lighted and lit the face of the C.O. I broke out,
"Herr Kommandant."

Editor: This chapter appears to be a statement taken from an
inmate at Dachau. Perhaps because of time restraints, it is poorly
organized and needs an introduction. It was given by a *woman*
with the initials E. H. and describes her experience at *Auschwitz*
not Dachau. What is historically significant is her claim to have
been a mistress of Auschwitz's commandant—the infamous
Rudolf Hoess—while a prisoner. (The commandant's name is
given as "Hoss" and "Hoess.") Whether her story is true or not,
those who heard her seem impressed by her sincerity and the
accuracy of details they could confirm. (Her description of Hoess
fits with his autobiography, *Commandant of Auschwitz.*) Note that
names and ranks appear confused. I have left the text unchanged,
but tried to resolve difficulties in footnotes and the index. (At the
end of this chapter, I have also added a table comparing military
ranks.) I felt that special care should be taken, since this is the
only historical mention many of these people will ever receive.

Bunker Clearings

I was detained nine months under special arrest in Bunker 11
in the men's camp. During this time I occupied various cells.
When I went to the door and spoke through the spy hole, I
could very easily talk to my cell neighbor; through this spy

hole I could also see a part of the corridor. In this way I got exact knowledge of what went on habitually in the "Bunker." For a long time I had as a neighbor Kurt Muller.[1] It was this man's job to do all the current secretarial work and to keep a list of prisoners up to date. One issue of this list went to the political section, the other remained in the prison. Regularly twice a week, usually Tuesday and Friday, a commission appeared. Sometimes there were delays, so that they sometimes came on Wednesday or Saturday. From 16th October 1942 to June 26th 1943 I believe I was under special arrest *"Komm. Arr."*[2] In all this time it happened only once that the commission was 12 days without coming.

This commission consisted of: SS Hauptstumfuhrer Aumeier,[3] SS Obersturmfuhrer Schwarz, SS Obersturmfuhrer Grabner, and secretaries of the political department. These changed. There was also SS Obersturmfuhrer Lachmann (I am not sure of this name). He usually wore mufti and a hunting hat. He also had a lame leg. His place was in the first of the political section. This Lachmann carried the list of Muller's in hand. They went from cell to cell and had them opened. I followed the process by ear and also watched through the peephole.

Each time a cell was opened, the prisoner had to give his name. Lachmann examined his list and struck the name off. It happened also that the prisoner was asked how long he was in *"Komm. Arrest."* It was always Aumeier who put this question, as he was chief of this group. I have never heard any other question being put. I have never heard a prisoner being questioned as to the reason of his arrest. Neither have I ever noticed that apart from Muller's list, they had any other

1. Kurt Muller was an inmate who served as a secretary in the same bunker where E. H. was held captive. He seems to have done his job so well that by page 86 he has acquired the rank of SS Rottenfuhrer (Corporal). This suggests that, despite the horrors of the camp, the line between victim and victimizer was not as fixed as some have assumed. Kurt Muller should not be confused with Kurt Mueller, an SS officer mentioned on page 78.
2. Editor: An abbreviation for *Kommandanturarrest*. In this statement the term is used in several different forms including K.A.
3. Editor: Hans Aumeier, who served under Hoess.

papers or files with them.

After the calling of the name, Hauptsturmfuhrer Aumeier shouted: "Stay in or come out." As the man came out, Aumeier decided "right" or "left." This indication was meant for two sentries of the polit. sect. [political section] who kept watch. These saw to it that the prisoners placed themselves correctly. Occasionally, Aumeier also said to a prisoner coming out: "I am sending in pension." Occasionally he also would start abusing them. His favorite term was "Bottle fly." The expression "Notified for punishment 1 or 2" I have never heard. Also I have never noticed any discussion about the prisoners among the members of the commission. Though I have noticed that when they had finished with one wing of the building, the names of those who were to stand to the right or the left were read through once more, Then usually new changes would take place from right to left and opposite.

By these changes there was some talk in the commission, but I could not hear what was being said; I soon noticed that the prisoners who were placed on the left were all sent for execution. I got to know it in this way, as those I know who were placed on the right used to send me regards from the camp, while I heard from the above-mentioned Muller that those who were placed on the left were shot. Once I saw the execution myself, from a cell on the courtyard side, where I was by accident. The men came naked in the yard and had to place themselves on four rows, one just behind the other, in front of the black wall and the face turned to it, The women kept their panties. Then the posts fired. It did not make much noise. The men fell into a heap. The next batch had to place themselves in front of them, and it went on like that till the day's work was over. Dr. Kitt attended these executions as physician. He was a tall spare man, and I am much mistaken if it was not Dr. Kitt. In one case he found that a man was still living. The sentry came back and gave him another shot in the neck. On the whole there were up to 40 prisoners at each execution. Sometimes there were only six or eight. The whole process of clearing out the Bunker went on fast; it lasted about half hour.

While prisoners were leaving one cell, the next was already opened. It is hard to say what reasons were there for the executions, though it struck me that prisoners who had escaped were always executed. Those men could be recognized by the fact that they were brought in without shoes or socks. I should say, under reserve, that the people executed in this clearing out were thoroughly healthy, powerful men of all ages up to 40. I have seldom seen sick or weak people. The sick, even late in the evening, were taken to hospital and nursed till restored to health. I can remember cases where such men, thoroughly cured, were then sent to be executed. For instance prisoner Gralla. He was a German from Kattowitz, a construction or mechanical engineer. I am myself a witness that Obersturmfuhrer Aumeier told him: "Ha, Mr. Gralla, I am sending to pension." Muller has also confirmed his death to me. This Gralla is not to be mistaken for his cousin, Dr. Gralla, who is still alive. Concerning the suppression of witnesses, I remember the following case: On Whitsunday 1942, a number of "capos" were arrested on a charge of jewel smuggling. Among them a prisoner whose Christian name was "Gustav." He worked, I believe, in a car or ammunition factory. I seem to remember that he was from Hanburg [probably Hamburg]. Age about 40, stature small, sagging. He had made statements against members of the SS and tried to get other prisoners to do the same.

These were very angry and would not do it. Two of them hanged themselves. The others were released and are at present soldiers. The talkative Gustav was shot. With these men was also a "capo," with Jugo as his Christian name, from the gipsy camp. He still talked to me shortly before Gustav was shot. The commission had then its usual membership. *Under reserve:* If I remember rightly the commanding officer, SS Obersturmbannfuhrer (Lieutenant Colonel) Hoss [Hoess] was at various times present at the process of clearing out the bunker. I can even remember one definite case. Sometime in March 1942 I heard then his voice in front of my cell door, and saw him through the peephole. While by all other clearing outs they also opened my cell, this time my door remained closed. I knocked on the door, so as to be able to speak to him. The door was not opened though. I only heard him ask: "How is H?" Later on Gehring told me that the C.O. showed great interest in me, but he would not open the door and he laughed derisively; witness of this case is the Pole, Maria M. who in those days shared my cell. I remember quite definitely that this took place at one of the usual clearing outs, and that I had followed the forming up of the men to right and left through my peephole. Obersturmfuhrer Schwarz was said to replace usually the C.O. of the commission, the procedure itself was supposed to be ordered from Berlin.

Executions of "Emigrants"

These "Bunker clearings" had nothing to do with other executions. So-called "emigrants" were also executed. These were men, women and even children of all ages. They came without exception late at night in the camp and were locked twelve and more in one-man cells. Once 15 women were locked in with me. They bore the traces of a long journey on them; they were dusty and dirty; they had luggage and crockery with them.

These entrances were not put down by Muller, the secretary, on his bunker's list. They also received special treatment, receiving for dinner a double ration and warm food: this never occurred in the camp. These transports, called in camp slang "got through or heavenwards" transports, were usually shot in the early morning at 4:30 or 5 a.m. before we arose.

The number of these transports varied between 120 and 150 people or more. Sometimes there also were smaller transports. I consider absolutely excluded that from these transports men were ever chosen to perform at first some work in the camp (postponement of execution). I have never noticed that either in the evening or the morning an interpreter was present to question those people who did not understand any German. Also in some cases they had to go through a quarantine cell on an upper floor, before they went in camp, or to go to Block 2. But this was never the case in my time. Moreover their whole luggage remained in the cell and was fetched after the execution. It never occurred that there was a choice made among this luggage. Apart from these executions, there were also so-called punishment executions. Should anything grave occur—an evasion was considered a grave enough case—then out of every team of workers a few would be taken out, without any sort of choice.

These men would be locked in, still in their working clothes, would not be put down on the entrance list and then on the morrow shot at 4:30 or 5. I can still remember that once a prisoner who worked as a chimney sweeper was locked in and shot then in his typical working clothes. Obersturmbannnfuhrer Grabner or Lachmann was always present at those executions.

Once I was myself taken to execution. Though I can't say with certainty if in this case it was a "clearing out." It was a Thursday at 8 or 8:30 a.m. I was sick and still asleep. In the cell with me were Maria M. and Regenscheidt. As I slept I hadn't heard whether other cells had been opened or not. Oberscharfuhrer Gehrige[4] appeared and said: "H, get ready, you are going to be shot." My two companions helped me dress. Outside in the corridor were 8 to 10 men, some of them in chains. Apart from Gehrige was a man called Porzel or some such name, nicknamed the "devil," a few members of the political section and a strikingly great number of sentries with rifles. We walked out of the prison building, down the camp alley, I at the head as the only woman. Suddenly Grabner and Aumeier who had not been there, met us. They were shocked at seeing me, and made everyone go back. I suppose we were on our way to the execution place No. 2 that lay near the former administrative buildings. Obersturmbannfuhrer Grabner called me an hour later and told me the whole thing was a joke of Oberscharfuhrer Gehrige.

Death certificates were made out for the men shot in the

---

4. Editor: This may be Oberscharfuhrer Gehring.

clearing out. As I was in charge of their effects, and had to send their belongings to the survivors, those documents came through my hands. For instance on a given day: 8:02 a.m. Miss X died of typhus; 8:07 a.m. Mrs. Y died of appendicitis. I remember exactly the case of three German girls, known to me, who were placed under arrest on the authority of the political section, and never came out, certainly did not go to the hospital, as we could make sure of. A certificate of natural death was made out for them. (I cannot remember at present the names of those concerned.) No mention was ever made for the reasons of their arrest. For the so-called emigrants such documents could not be established, because the prison only placed the people from transport in the cells but did not have their names. At any rate, so Muller assured me.

Other Means of Killing

Apart from shooting in "*Kommandantur Arrest*," there were also hunger, thirst and injections. While I occupied a cell close to the "standing cell," or was myself in the standing cell, the following German citizens died of hunger: Herbert Roman, Heinrich Roman (they were not related), Bruno Graf and an "Obercapo" from the ammunition factory.

Herbert Roman was from Hamburg. The following charge was laid against him: he had gone with a car into the women's camp to take a load of corpses and had taken this opportunity to meet a girl from Hamburg, Margot Schmidt. Heinz Roman was supposed to know something of an attempted murder against an SS sentry. The capo from the ammunition factory was supposed to have helped four Poles to escape. Bruno Graf was supposed to have robbed one chicken. These prisoners received food at first, then every fourth day, at the end neither food nor drinks or the possibility of going to the toilet.

It was a real torture to hear them complaining of thirst all through the night. The Capo died first after some 14 days. Then Bruno Graf died after he had been hung by the arms for five hours in the sun. Then followed Heinz Roman and at last Herbert Roman who held out for 40 days. I supposed that the men who spent the night in the standing cell, and who worked all day long, could at least get him some water. H. Sturmbannfuhrer Aumeier and Obersturmfuhrer Grabner stood often in front of the standing cell.

I often begged them, at least to liberate those Germans from their sufferings, but Hauptsturmfuhrer Aumeier answered: "The hounds must die." Obersturmfuhrer [Grabner] on the contrary remained quiet. After their death I suffered great anxiety, because I had always in my ears their voices, complaining and at the end reduced to a whisper. Also the state of frightful thinness, with long hair and beard, their corpses were terrible to look at. I saw this when they dragged a corpse on the ground past my cell door.

Gehring quietened me later and gave me cigarettes. By this he only wanted to probe my mind and learn if the others had told me anything or told me to speak about it. He also said: "There is no regret to be had about this lad, he was a great criminal."

I myself witnessed once how Oberscharfuhrer Gehring killed a German, who I do not know by name, with one single blow in the stomach or near the heart. A Polish M.D. was busy placing a bandage on me, as I saw this, and saw the man carried away dead. The physician came back then and just said: "Out."

The injections were mainly carried out by a medical service man from the surgery section by the name of Heini. Once or twice a month he came to the school. There the prisoners were shown to him. Those had swollen feet, either from running barefoot or from the climate, were called out to the row.

After the other[s] had gone to work, he gave them injections, whereupon they fell dead. No doctor was present either at the injections or the death. Heini acted quite independently.

While I was in the K.A., two Czeck [Czech] girls came temporarily into my cell. Both were called out one day and brought into the next cell. There they received from two SS I did not know but from what they said, from the political direction, each an injection. Death followed at once, I had never seen those two SS in the camp previous to this. The reasons for this [these] actions are unknown to me. Before I camt [came] to the bunker, I was myself a witness to Heini administering injections to four women and the four babies they carried at arm. Also here, death was immediate. This happened in the women's hospital.

The "Buddy" Riot

In September 1942 a riot broke out in "Buddy" (nickname given to the school) between German and Jewish prisoners. All the Jewish women, 93 of them, were killed by the German women. They struck them down sith [with] stools, tables, boards or anything that came handy. Next day they lad [lay] dead in the camp alley near "Buddy."[5]

The SS guard reported the proceeding to SS Hauptst. Fuhrer Schwartz who carried out the inquest. The Germans said they feared the Jewesses would kill them, as the previous night the Jewesses had tried to kill the German woman. To the question "who killed the Jewesses?" nobody answered at first.

Then the SS said they would not be punished if they reported themselves, as they were only Jews. Also a prospect of liberation was dangled before their eyes, if they reported themselves. They went in the K.A. On October 16th I came myself in the K.A. The next day I spoke with the girls. They told me the whole story. They were told they would go to the artificial rubber works. They told me more about the riot; the chief of the Block of the punishment company (I can't remember his name at the present) had incited them to kill the Jews, and the SS had helped them to do it. They also told me that the night of the riot, the SS guards had thrown tiles

---

5. Hoess mentioned a "Budy blood-bath" in his autobiography on page 135. Budy was a punishment camp located about five miles from Auschwitz. Its workers were employed in drainage work, and its Capos were recruited from criminals in the camp. Hoess noted: "I find it incredible that human beings could ever turn into such beasts." It was an odd remark given what he did every day.

on the Jews. A few days later, these girls were fetched suddenly at 5:30 or 6, and were brought to chief of block 11 of the K.A. There each of them received an injection. "Injection Heini" and two other SS I did not know were present. I cannot say with certainty if Hauptsturmfuhre Aumeier or Hauptsturmfuhrer Schwarz were also there. One of the two was there, which, I am not sure.

I was accidently [accidentally] in the next room, being bandaged and got knowledge of the case in this way. The block chief was temporarily arrested and then released again. Nothing further happened in this case. "Injection Heini" whose name I do not know, has a face like a monkey, he walks with head bent, shoulders high, average stature. The prisoner Aurelia Reichert, No. 501, chief of the *Revier*, can give further information on this case. Also the Jewish chief M.D. whose Christian name was Enna. She was a protegee of Dr. Rode. It has been said that Dr. Rode gave the orders for these injections. Various pictures were now presented to me. They were pictures of the prisoner Herbert Roman.

(Note of the instructor [interrogator]: Mrs. H did recognize the prisoner Herbert Roman without doubt, as the various photos were presented to her. This Herbert Roman is the man that died from starvation.)

Books of the *Kommandanturarrest*

The two official books of the K.A. were now presented to me to help my memory. After long consideration I must declare that these books are not the original books of the K.A. I have seen the originals myself. It was twice as big as the two copy books put one against the other and three or four fingers thick. The covering is black or dark blue. Also the two copy books are not complete. The women, who were always in great numbers in the K.A., were not mentioned. Many men were also missing, for instance one Franz Kummel, who was twice in the K.A. towards the end of my detention, that is June 1943. He was block chief in the K.A. Further, I remember prisoners of whom I only remember the Christian name, and which are not written down, for instance Hugo, Franz and Hannes (calfactor in the K.A.). Hannes and Franz were locked up because they had at night opened up the cells of the K.A. to permit to the male prisoners sexual intercourse with the women. As I heard this happened because the three SS of the K.A., successors to Gehring (possibly it was Gehring himself) took part in this sexual intercourse.

In the case of the above-mentioned Gralla, the death mark, a cross, is missing in the copy book. Names of other prisoners have now come back to me: the men killed by Gehring is Walter Walterscheidt, No. 15476. He is recorded as a case of suicide by poison on 23.3.43.

The case of the suppression of a witness is Gustav Vaupel. The prisoners mentioned in the first copy book under the number[s] from 124549 to 124567, arrival date 9th of June 1943, 6:30 p.m., are the prisoners who on the next day at 11:30 a.m. were shot as a reprisal. The exit date with 2:30 p.m. is false.

The above-mentioned chimney sweep is Stanislaus Bialke. The dead cross behind his name is also missing. I remember further that one of the prisoners who in my time died on [of] starvation in the bunker was a German, Erich Klose by name, No. 19860. He belonged to those who were involved in a jewel case. This was said to be a purely SS matter.

Other list which have stuck on the K.A. list are: Bruno Brodniewica, a German citizen, camp-chief, brought in on December 30th, 1942, liberated on March 25th, 1943. He disappeared after he left the bunker. Officially he was gone to Muhlhausen. The rumor was spread in the camp that he was killed because he knew too much. He occupied once a cell next to mine. I talked with hin [him] and he told me without giving details that, that he knew all about the terrific goings-on in the camp, and was arrested because he knew too much.

His successor (Ludwig was his Christian name) disappeared also. He was brought in, I believe, in June or July 1944 by Hauptsturmf. Schwarz. The disappearance of a Jewish M.D., Samuel Mishki, belongs to the same type; he worked with Prof. Glanberg,[6] thanks to special Berlin recommendations. He appeared one day in the K.A. then was directly taken by ambulance to the crematory and killed there. His name is not in the copy book. As witness against Hauptsturmfuhrer Tauber (captain), the prisoner Richard Faustmann, No. 113666, may be called. He was brought in by Tauber himself. I have not found either in the copybook the names of Heinz, Willy and the third from the clothes depot Canada,[7] who was brought in in April/May 1943 and shot.

Hauptscharfuehrer Gehring, administrator of the arrest place, struck the prisoners with fists and keys. During winter, he would compel prisoners to go naked in the courtyard, to take exercises. When they were well warmed up, he gave them a shower with a hose. I witnessed myself one of these cases, as I by chance was washing at the time. Once in February an M.D., presumably Dr. Kitt, came up and had Gehring immediately arrested. Gehring confessed to me once about those ill-treatments, that for all he did, he had orders from the political section, and mentioned the name of Lachmann. I doubt just now whether it is really Lachmann (a small chap, with a game leg) and not the criminal Secretary Wosnitza. SS Unterscharfuehrer Kurt Mueller[8] could be called as a witness against Gehring.

Untersharrfuehrer (sergeant) Stiebitz, was known as the greatest petticoat hunter in the camp. It was his charge to take the men to the brothel. The prisoners concerned, who were with me in the hospital, such as Hilde Goltz, Anneliese, Peter. The above-mentioned Sonja Regenscheidt complained that he would peep at them during the sexual intercourse.

---

6. Editor: This may be Prof. Glauberg.
7. Editor: Canada was the name of the camp depot where clothing and other items from those killed were sorted for shipment back to Germany.
8. Editor: This Kurt Mueller has the rank of Sergeant. In the pages that follow, there is mention of an Obersturmfuehrer (First Lieutenant) Mueller (p. 80) and a SS Hauptsturmfuehrer (Captain) Mueller (p. 81). In the index I assume that this Mueller has risen through the ranks from Sergeant to Captain. It is faintly possible that the Kurt *Mueller* mentioned here is the Kurt *Muller* first mentioned on page 68 who has the rank of corporal on page 87. In that case, Mueller's first name is unknown.

Hauptsturmfuehrer Schwarz was also mentioned as equally curious. Stiebetz had an affair with the prisoner Annemarie Goerlitz. They once had a rendezvous in the clothes store-room, and Oberscharfuehrer Tauber told me I must not tell this to anyone. I was present myself when Obersturmfuehrer (Lt.) Grabner warned Annemarie Goerlitz. He added, "If it happens again you'll just see . . . !" She was then sent, with her hair cut, to Ravensbruck. It was generally known in the camp that Stiebitz had intimate relations with a Jewish secretary, Iberia Katja. This girl was also involved in the prosecution against Unterscharfuehrer Pallitsch, who celebrated orgies in the gipsy camp and was on this account condemned by the tribunal of Breslau, thanks to Stiebitz. Katja was fetched out of the bunker after she had been six hours there. She pretends actually to be Aryan, but she came to the camp of Jews, and I have seen myself her Jewish identification papers. I also know her Jewish brothers, who live in Birkenau.

As to other names, I also know Unterscharfuehrer Heueer. He was the man who interrogated and struck Hild Logauer, Regenscheidt, etc., on the Stalin swing.

SS Oberscharfuehrer (sergeant major) Boger[9] called himself with relish "the Devil." Formerly I have called him Porgel. He also had this name in the camp. As I had been released two or three days from K.A., Boger called me. He asked, "Do you know me?" I answered "Yes." "What is my name?" he asked. He then added, "I am the devil." He then asked me why I was interested in the Jewess Zimmerspitz. He struck me with full power under the chin and in the face, so that I tumbled down.

Commandant Hoess and E.H.

SS Obsturmfuehrer. I already met the C.O. as I was brought in Auschwitz. He or the Hauptsturmfuehrer Schwarz used to ask the newcomers if there were typists amongst them, what-

---

9. Editor: This may be Wilhelm Boger, responsible for some 1,000 murders at Auschwitz. He was transferred to Auschwitz in December 1942 and was soon in charge of the camp's "escape department."

ever their profession. I gave mine as a helper of a drugstore. The M.D., Van Brodemann wanted to have me for the hospital. Obersturmfuehrer Hoess then let secretary Langenfels give me a room all to myself in Block 4. A few days later I was ordered by Obersturmfuehrer Mueller to the C.O. because an artisan was wanted. I was received in the house by the C.O.'s wife, who in the hall showed me a carpet and asked me if I could mend it. I undertook the job and worked at it for two days. During this time I often saw the C.O. coming and going. He asked me if I were H. and put no other question to me. He remarked that properly he should not employ a political prisoner in his house, but his wife had various jobs for me. I then prepared two tapestries, a tapestry cushion in silk, a car rug and various blankets. I liked to work in the C.O.'s house, as far as keeping up of the entrance lists allowed me the time. I still spent the night in camp. As long as I worked in the house, I was fed there. I ate alone in a room and the same food as the C.O. himself.[10]

The food consisted of soup, entree, meat, vegetables, and pastries or cakes, fruit salad and coffee. It was extremely good and compared favorably with the menu of a big hotel in peace time. The two Jewish tailor girls (whose names I forget) who worked in the house got the same food. One of them is still alive. I talked with her a few days before I was sent to Munich. These two girls worked from 1942 onwards, until three or four months ago, uninterruptedly in the C.O.'s house. Where the C.O. or his wife secured this amazing quantity of material or clothes, I don't know, as the C.O.'s wife went very plainly dressed, one could say almost too plainly dressed. The C.O. soon took a special interest in me. It did not strike me at first, but my fellow prisoners soon drove to my notice to the fact that the C.O. was strikingly interested in me. The C.O. had me called to him each time he came in the camp, or he came himself to the place where I worked.

10. In his autobiography, Hoess claimed that: "No former prisoner can ever say that he was in any way or at any time badly treated in our house. My wife's greatest pleasure would have been to give a present to every prisoner who was in any way connected with our household." (p. 156)

He talked of business, but laughed at the same time in a particular way. I answered in the same way because I must confess that I liked him as a man. Apart from the frequent business talks, he did all he could to favor me and make my detention lighter. In the first room I occupied there were three other women. As the C.O. learned this, he ordered Hauptsturmfuehrer Aumeier to prepare a special room for me on the floor of Block 4. I could decorate this with my own furniture and real carpets. On weekends I got a furlough on parole and could also move about freely in the town of Auschwitz and could stay out the night. In these cases I used to sleep in the buildings of the staff, outside the camp. The C.O. also saw me often smoke, which was forbidden to prisoners, and never said anything. When I wanted to hide the cigarette, he told me not to trouble. I also got permission to have a personal cook and a maid for my personal needs. Witness for this is SS Hauptsturmfuehrer Aumeier. On my birthday, a special feast was organized for me in the C.O.'s house. The people in camp believed at first that I was related to the C.O. and asked me about it.

The C.O. expressed his particular feelings for me for the first time as in May 1942, his wife being out, I was in his villa, sitting by the radio. Without a word, he came to me and gave me a kiss. I was surprised and frightened, escaped him and locked myself up in the toilet. There were too many obstacles between him and me on account of his position and the fact that he was married. From then on, I did not come in the C.O.'s house any more. I reported myself as sick and tried to hide from him when he asked for me. Though he succeeded time and again in finding me, on this [these] occasions, he did not talk of the kiss. I was only twice more in his house before my birthday, by order. Then once on my birthday. Then he sent the SS Hauptsturmfuehrer Mueller to tell me that I was free on Sunday and I should bathe, have my hair dressed, put on my best clothes and call on his wife on Sundays. At the end of September his wife told me I need not come any more for the time being, as the C.O. was sick in Bielitz and she was with him. Two or three days later, the

Supervisor Drechsel took the work away from me.

A fortnight later, I was sent to the S.L. As reason, I was told I had committed some infraction in the C.O.'s house. Thereupon I wrote a letter to the C.O., another to his wife and another to his cook, the prisoner Sophie Stippl. In these, I explained the facts and asked them to take no account of rumors and to do something for me. As an answer, the next day at 1:30 p.m. I was transferred to the *Kommandanturarrest*. This was on October 16, 1942. On this day, I should have entered the hospital as Chemist, because a month before the deputy SS head M.D. had come in the camp and had hinted at my liberation and removal to a hospital on the East Front. I pointed out that on account of my long detention, my nerves wouldn't stand it. Then the M.D. said that I must work in the SS Hospital in Auschwitz. I was to train at once in the prisoners' hospital before I went into quarantine. Still on the same day, about 8:30 p.m., Injection Heini came to fetch me. I refused to work with Jewesses and remarked that I needed no training. Then came the SS Obersturmfuehrer Kraetzer and said I could spend my quarantine in camp, as I was quite healthy anyhow. During this four weeks quarantine in camp, I should train nurse, prisoner, Gerturd Malorny. This I did. I was brought to the K.A. by supervisor Hasse. As we passed by the sentry, she told him: "this one shall not come back." No one could or would give me the reasons for my arrest.

Until January 1943, I was quite well in K.A. Usually I had a one-person cell, provided with a good bed and mattress. I had a table and a stool, could read, write and smoke. I wrote two or three times to the C.O., through the political direction (SS Obersturmfurhrer Grabner), and asked for the reason of my detention. I never got an answer. During this time, SS Hauptsturmfuehrer Aumeier, SS Hauptsturmfuehrer Schwarz and SS Obersturmfuehrer Grabner came occasionally to see me. They told me my case depended directly upon the C.O. I was all right. And then they would laugh.

The Relationship turns Sexual

According to my recollection, on December 16, 1942, about 11

P.M. I was already asleep, suddenly the C.O. appeared before me. I hadn't heard the opening of my cell and was such frightened. It was dark in the cell. I believed at first it was an SS man or a prisoner and said, "What is this tomfoolery, I forbid you." Then I heard "Pst," and a pocket lamp was lighted and lit the face of the C.O. I broke out, *"Herr Kommandant."* Then we were both silent a long time. As I had composed myself, I thought something evil was afoot and asked: "What is wrong?" Then Hoess spoke his first words, "You are coming out." I asked, "Now, at once?" He answered once more, "Pst. Be very quiet, we'll talk it over" and sat at the foot of my bed. I reminded him I had written to him and why didn't I get an answer, and why was I under arrest? He didn't answer this, but asked if I wasn't all right, he had done everything to improve my condition, and did I need anything. Then he moved up slowly from the end of the bed and tried once more to kiss me. I defended myself and made some noise. He then warned me to be quiet, nobody knew he was there. I asked him how he had come in, and if no one had seen him. He told me he had come through the garden door and had unlocked the door himself.

I was again very irritated and told him that my liberation from prison had been arranged for the 16th of October and that I should have been working for a long time in the SS hospital. He answered that my liberation was approved, but he did not know that I was supposed to work in the SS hospital. He answered that he would first have to look in the Acts, because he had been ill and this was his first time back in the camp, and he came directly to me. I asked him then why he came at night. I told him that he could see me during the day in the *Kommandanteure.* I did not lose the idea of being executed. The SS Obersturmbannfuhrer Hoss [Hoess] told me I could be quite unconcerned. I was under his protection and he only came to talk alone without disturbing me.

He asked me then why I was always so reserved with him. I told him that as *Kommandant,* he was for me a respectful personality and that he was married. He said then I should not worry, that he knew what he was doing. He requested me to be his friend. Then he tried again to kiss me and was somewhat sweeter. During all that time I was very anxious, listening and looking at the door that was open, because I could not forget that somebody was staying outside. The *Kommandant* was not allowed to go alone in the camp. Therefore I could not believe that he came alone to me. I insisted again that he should go away. Finally he went away and told me that I should think about it and that he would come back. I said then, "But please not during the night." He closed the door very quietly and one could hear the noise of boots from cell 26 where I was. I did not hear the outer gate close or the front door. These doors were always shut during the night.

Two nights later, again a few minutes after 11 o'clock as he had told me, he came again. He asked me if I had made a decision. I said, "No, I didn't want to," and I told him, "All I wanted was to be released." He said then that he had prepared everything. He had arranged a nice room in a very beautiful house. To my question as to when I would finally be released, he answered that I would see it very soon. Then we had a very long talk for two hours on personal questions. He did not say anything about himself. He asked me about my life and my family situation, which were not in my records. At the end he tried again to be friendly. I resisted and made him wait saying that the door was open and that somebody could always come. He said that I should not worry, that nobody would come. I didn't let that influence me, and he went away in a nasty temper.

The following day was Sunday. In the morning he made a Bunker inspection. Then I had to go in another cell that one could open and shut from the inside. It was, if I remember correctly, Cell #6. Some days later, he came again during the night. He asked then if he should go away. I said "no." He asked me what I had to say. I told him he knew what I had to say. Then he came to me in bed, and we had sexual intercourse.

Some days later he came again. This time he undressed himself completely. At midnight there was [an] alarm. I think something was on fire somewhere in camp. Outside in the hall the light was turned on. One could hear the steps of Gehring. Hoss [Hoess] hid himself naked in the corner behind the door, and I hid the uniform in bed. During these moments the light went on a short time. Gehring looked through the spyhole and put the light out immediately. When everything was quiet, Hoss [Hoess] put his clothes on and went outside but came back soon and said he could not go out of the camp because there was too much movement. He stayed then with me until after one o'clock.

The following times he did not undress again. He just made himself comfortable. All in all we had four or five nights of sexual intercourse. His interest in me did not seem to lag. We had later still some conversations together. I brought up the subject of my liberation once again. He said I had to have patience. He had started an inquiry against the Superintendent, Miss Hartman.

When he came to me the following time, I asked occasionally what would happen to me if he was discovered. He said I ought to deny it and asked me if I would do it. I swore silence. He gave me then the advice, if more was asked, to say that a prisoner had come to me. I replied that I did not know any prisoners. He thought he knew that more SS men and nice looking Capos had interest for me. Then he asked what I had with Flichtinger [Fichtinger]. I told him that he had written me and that I had answered him telling him not to annoy me. Then he asked if it was an affair of a nice Capo. I described him as being small and not completely to my taste. His advice was then that I should indicate Fichtinger. I did not like to indicate Fichtinger, but he thought I could do it quietly. For me nothing would happen if I had relations with a prisoner. He took a sheet of paper out of his notebook, and I had to give him, in the light of his flashlight, a written declaration that I had acquaintance with the prisoner Frans Fichtinger. This paper he put in a small leather book. Hoss [Hoess] did not give me anything, but he lost once by me the strap of his gloves. A strap with a button where the Nappa is. This strap I keep in my luggage.

Those conversations were the occasion that, during the night of the fire, the prisoner SS man Eduard Lockhauser-baumer who was in a cell near to mine (*prisoners presence there subsequently checked in prison files*) heard the sound of the boots on the pavement and looked outside his cell and saw Hoss [Hoess], but he had taken him for Obersturmfuhrer Schwarz. He spoke to me about him from cell to cell.

E. H. Becomes Pregnant

During his last visit, the *Kommandant* said he wanted to come back to me. But soon afterwards at the beginning of February I had a very severe attack. Always before it had gone away. I thought it was a gallstone attack. This diagnosis was confirmed by Dr. Stassel, *Bunkerdoctor*. In the evening I had a second attack with terrible vomiting. Then the prisoners' doctor came, Dr. Doring. After examination he told me carefully, "You are pregnant." The following day he came again and examined me thoroughly. He established the fact definitely that I was pregnant eight weeks. He asked me who was the man. I told him I could not answer and asked him not to say anything about it. I urged him at the same time to help me. Therefore, the following day a janitor at the Bunker, I think Teresiak, handed me through the window two medicines. I took one. As I got terrible pains, I threw the second away. Dr. Doring did not come anymore.

After this attempt at abortion I was taken into a special cell of the dungeon, which is a small dark hole and only very little air can pass into it. Otherwise it was quite dark. One can just stand in that hole or stay on the knees to have a change of the position.

The next morning, when Gehring came to fetch me, I was completely naked as I had been washing. Just as I was finishing, Gehring took me along; he only allowed me to put on an apron. Witness of this is Rottenfuhrer Muller. I had to stay in the above described cell all the time. I was not told the reason. When I was in the dungeon, I got terribly afraid and started crying for which Hannes had to pour several buckets of water on me. The reason why I cried so terribly was because there was a dead body in the cell which I could feel in the darkness.

I was taken out of that cell and was put into the next one. As I continued crying, once more several buckets of water were poured on me. The first days, I received the normal quantity of internees' food. After that I only got some bread and coffee and each fourth day I received some cooked food. For a period of nine weeks I had no possibility to wash myself, and the last 17 days there was no using the W.C. I had to do this in my cell.

During the imprisonment I asked Rottenfuhrer Muller to bring me some clothes as I felt very cold. He advised me to talk to Gehring. Gehring turned up several times, opened the little hole and called "old cow, hysterical goat," when I asked him for a drop of water. He expressed surprise several times that I had not died yet.

(Note of interrogator: while talking of these things she became rather excited. One can clearly see how terrible the reminder of this time affects her.)

As far as I can remember it must have been winter time when I was in that cell because Gehring gave orders to cut off the steam heat for my cell. About that time also, Obersturmfuhrer Grabner and Hauptsturmfuhrer Aumeier were in front of my cell. The door of my cell was not quite closed, which enabled me to see those two. I could also hear that they spoke in front of Herman Roman's cell and when Roman asked them to save his life, Aumeier just replied, "you will die you dog." I had to vomit and felt better after that.

After my release from this special cell, I asked the neighbor of the next cell how to manage an abortion. This was about April or May in 1943. Miss (Mrs.) Regenscheidt told me to get hold of a long needle with which I should open the ovary and put green soap inside. The above-mentioned Kurt Muller brought me those things along as I told him I needed it for my washing. With the support of a mirror I started trying it with the result that I lost a lot of blood and the spot became rather swollen. The whole trial was without any result.

I believe it was the 26 of June when I was released, the very same day when the execution of the Jewess Zimmerspitz took place. When Aumeier gave the order to get out, I also entered the corridor. Obersturmfuhrer Grabner, when he saw me, said, "for heavens sake that is N," and I was sent back into the cell. To Aumeier he said, "she will be sent back into the camp." This order was given by the commander. She will be sent to Buddy as *Blockalteste* (in charge of a barracks).

Instead of that I was sent back into the punishment company where Oberscharfuhrer Tauber received me. He said I got here by special order of the commander and would have all advantages. I got into the hospital, where I received something which managed the abortion. In the punishment company I was allowed then to stay in bed for ten or twelve days.

Her Pregnancy Investigated

After my convalescence I worked three months as a janitress. After that I was in charge of the kitchen and had to go into the hospital again on account of bronchitis. Before my release I got typhus. Ever since I am in the hospital waiting to be transferred to Munich.

On the 12th of July I was supposed to be sent to Munich as the whole hospital was cleared out. That was in 1944. Only five old Jewish women and myself stayed. Obersturmfuhrer Hessler intended to put me in the dungeon until I was sent to Munich. When I refused, he got [an] order from the commander that I will be taken into the new barracks for the time being.

While there the civilian employee, Dr. Gobel, of the Glauberg station, gave the order that I shall have to be sent to Birkenau for gas. In fact I was put together with the other Jewish women into the car, but in the very last moment the SS man in charge of the Glauberg station came and gave [an] order to bring me back again. The clerk of the hospital office, the internee Adolf Laatsch, assured me that Dr. Gobel put my name as the first one on the list of those who are going to pass the gas chambers.

I still have to point out that, in the presence of Prof. Glauberg and the Camp Commander, I had to meet Dr. Doring. Nobody else was present. I was asked whether I knew Dr. Doring. This question was put to me by the Camp Commander, Mr. Baer. Dr. Doring gave me a sign not to say anything and answered, "No, I do not know this woman," and I agreed that I did not know him. After this meeting I immediately said to Prof. Glauberg and the doctors that I did recognize Dr. Doring. Prof. Glauberg asked me why I did not say so before. I replied that I did not know the purpose of this meeting, and Dr. Doring immediately had said that he did not know me. Fifteen minutes later I wrote a note to Commander Hoss [Hoess] telling him about the meeting and declaration. A second note, which I sent to the Commander, said that Prof. Glauberg refused to take me into the new station, and I asked for orders from him.

Two or three days later, Hauptscharfuhrer Klausen was sent to me by the Commander to ask me whom I gave those letters to, as he did not receive same. Klausen advised me to hand him all the letters which I wanted to send to the Commander, so as to be sure that they would reach their destination. After that I was asked by the Commander to state any special wishes I had about food. I was allowed to write them on a list. I did so, and it was signed for agreement by the Commander.

The meeting with the Commander Hoss [Hoess] in the presence of the SS Judge Untersturmfuhrer Wiebeck took place as follows: I was asked by Wiebeck what enabled me to say that the Commander knew who was with me in the dungeon. I laughed, and the Commander said that this was quite unclear to him. He got rather excited and put his hand on the bed to steady himself. He confirmed also that I behaved very decently, and that I had been kept in the dungeon for my own protection. He did not know anything as to why I was kept in that little hole. To the contrary, he accused him [me] for not having said anything to him about that. When I was told that in January 1943 Hoss [Hoess] refused my release from camp on account of very bad behavior, I did not have any declaration for that.

About the fears which I had in connection with my transfer to Munich, I spoke to my fiancée, the already mentioned Fichtinger. He advised me under all circumstances not to mention the commander's name. I was also careful enough to put myself under psychiatric care for a period of six weeks. The certificate about this from the Polish camp doctor, as well as the written diaries about everything that happened, are in the possession of Fichtinger.

I also want to say that once I listened to a talk between several internees, the names of whom I do not know. They said that they were keeping a hiding place together with some SS men where they got some very valuable things: foreign money, gold and silver, which they want to take along after the clearing out of Camp Auschwitz. Some of that staff was supposed to be in a house, which was left alone and was situated on the way to Hamense. I myself know the house by talk, but I do not know where in this area the stuff is kept. The other part of those valuable things are supposed to be underneath Block No. 2 in the men's camp.

Waste of Textiles

The textiles were stored in several barracks of which I only know two. Those have been cleared out. Those barracks were full to the ceiling with clothes, furs, suitcases, bags and boots. All those things were kept there for such a long time and without any care being taken that the rats spoiled them until they become unusable, with the result that they had to load all that stuff on trucks and carry it to the crematorium to be burned. Hauptscharfuhrer Effinger was responsible for that. He used to always drink and fool around with women all the time. When I left Auschwitz, the textiles were stored in stone buildings, and the intern in charge told me the same thing was happening as it did before. I saw them burn great hills of valuable suitcases, leatherware, and boots which were spoiled from the wetness.

Ravensbruck

I have been in Ravensbruck as from the 5/12/41 until 24/3/42 [5 December 1941 to 24 March 1942]. During that time I saw many cases of cruelty and very bad treatment against internees. I saw the head woman guard, Mandel, when she sent dogs against the internees. Those internees were wounded and immediately sent into the punishment company. No care was taken about them and the majority died there on account of their own wounds. Fifty-seven of the 1000 internees who were transferred from Ravensbruck to Auschwitz were still alive at the time of my departure. Those 57 can be used as witnesses.

The political department of Ravensbruck was supposed to have a special cell in the dungeon into which no air could come. Internees who would not confess were kept in here. Slowly water was let in it and when it was right up to the head, the internee would [be] ask[ed] through the little hole once more if they would confess. If he refused, more water was let in until he drowned. Irmgard Ludwig who is still alive offered herself as a witness. She said that she had seen a dead body floating in the cell. Also the internee who had to do all the cleaning in the dungeon and was transferred with me to Auschwitz, told me when we were together in the hospital that things were like that. She also said that there was a guard woman named Mandel who used to beat internees in the cells after some cloth was put in front of the eyes to keep them from seeing.

Editor: This chapter continues the CIC report begun in Chapter 3 and completed in the appendices that follow. This section was originally entitled "Statement of E. H." Note that the original only had the last two subheadings. The other subheadings have been added, along with additional paragraph breaks and punctuation to make the narrative easier to follow. (In the original, one single-spaced, typed paragraph was almost three pages long.) In addition, to assist the reader, I have added to the original text the following table comparing German military ranks with their equivalents in the U.S. Army.

Table 1: Comparative Ranks During WWII

SS	SA	German Army	U.S. Army
Mann		Schütze	Private
Sturmmann		Oberschütze	Private 1st Class
Rottenfuehrer		Gefreiter	Corporal
Unterscharfuehrer		Unteroffizier	Sergeant
Scharfuehrer		Unterfeldwebel	Staff Sergeant
Oberscharfuehrer		Feldwebel	Technical Sergeant
Hauptscharfuehrer		Oberfeldwebel	Master Sergeant
Stabsscharfuehrer		Hauptfeldwebel	Sergeant Major
Sturmscharfuehrer		Stabsfeldwebel	Sergeant Major
Untersturmfuehrer	Sturmfuehrer	Leutnant	2d Lieutenant
Obersturmfuehrer	Obersturmfuehrer	Oberleutnant	1st Lieutenant
Hauptsturmfuehrer	Hauptsturmfuehrer	Hauptmann	Captain
Sturmbannfuehrer	Sturmbannfuehrer	Major	Major
Obersturmbann-fuehrer	Obersturmbann-fuehrer	Obersleutnant	Lieutenant Colo-nel
Standartenfuehrer	Standartenfuehrer	Oberst	Colonel
Oberfuehrer	Oberfuehrer		a senior Colonel
Brigadefuehrer	Brigadefuehrer	Generalmajor	Brigadier General
Gruppenfuehrer	Gruppenfuehrer	Generalleutnant	Major General
Obergruppenfue-hrer	Obergruppenfue-hrer	General der Infan-terie, etc.	Lieutenant General
Oberstgruppenfue-hrer		Generaloberst	General
Reichsfuehrer	Stabschef	Generalfeldmar-schall	General of the Army

A

Special Case Reports

Some of the more outstanding case reports are summarized below:

Schilling, Kurt Karl, Dr.

Dr. Schilling was apprehended by this detachment to ascertain his connection with the various medical experimental stations of the camp. He retired from the practice of medicine in 1932. He had been, for many years, Professor of Parasitology [Parasitology] at the Medical School of the University of Berlin, and for the past 20 years had been particularly interested in malaria. In 1936, he was summoned by a Dr. Conti, Minister of Health, to appear personally before Himmler. Schilling stated he was ordered by Himmler to proceed to the Dachau Concentration Camp for the purpose of research in an attempt to find a method of specifically immunizing individuals against malaria. This he did since 1936, and in this period of time he inoculated some 2,000 people with malaria.

Wiebeck, Gerhard

Subject is an SS judge holding the rank of SS Obersturmfuhrer. Subject is a lawyer by profession and in this capacity secured employment with the State Police in Berlin, where he remained until 1940. In 1939, he attained the rank of Untersturmfuhrer in the Allgemeine SS because of his position on the Help Crimes Commission. In February 1940, Wiebeck was transferred to Waffen SS as a soldier in Prague, and became an SS judge in November 1943. As an SS judge, subject was charged with investigation of all crimes committed by SS men and from this point of view has much information to offer concerning SS men.

Welter, Wilhelm—SS Oberscharfuhrer

Subject became member of the NSDAP and the SA in 1932. He joined the SS Totenkopf unit, Dachau in 1935. Welter was *Arbeitsdienstfuhrer* in the concentration camp. He was very brutal and was accused of killing many prisoners and prisoners of war. For one-half year, subject was also in charge of the Friedrichshafen branch of the Dachau Concentration Camp. In 1945, during an interview with SS General Pohl[1] on the camp grounds, he was transferred to the Russian front, consequently wounded and returned to Germany to train the HJ Birgsau, Allgue. From there he made a trip to Dachau on 7 May 1945, and was apprehended 9 May 1945. Subject's interrogation revealed the hideout place of 300 higher SS officers in the mountains.

Schuster, Heinrich Johann

Subject was an inmate of the Auschwitz Concentration Camp from 1942 to January 1945. There he assisted the SS doctors in the hospital wards. He was accused of singling out other internees for the gas chamber despite the fact that he had only studied for three and a half years and was not a doctor.[2] In January 1945, he was transferred to the Dachau Concentration Camp, where he again volunteered to work in the hospital. Schuster was arrested after transferring back from the hospital to the camp ground while he was trying to mingle with the other internees.

Bottger, Franz—SS Hauptscharfuhrer

Rapportfuhrer in the camp, subject is an outstanding example of inhuman cruelty and brutality. He participated in the killing of many political prisoners as well as the killing of many prisoners of war. On 27 April 1945, he left Dachau with an evacuation transport. Over 1200 people were killed on the way. Subject was recognized and apprehended by infor-

---

1. Editor: General Oswald Pohl ran the work program for camp inmates. His responsibilities included the melting down of gold taken from Jews. He was executed in 1951

2. Editor: Of course, completing medical school would not have made his "singling out" for the gas chambers any less abhorrent.

mants working for this detachment about 30 kilometers distance from Dachau.

Kick, Johann—SS Untersturmfuhrer

Former chief of the Political Department of the Dachau Concentration Camp, head of the STAPO Aussenstelle Dachau, Kick related that he entered the Political Department of the Dachau Concentration Camp on 20 May 1937 as a hearer of cases, and that in January 1938, he was named Chief of the department by SS Sturmfuhrer Beck, *Oberregierungsrat* of the Gestapo, Munich. He held this position until August 1944, when he was put in charge of STAPO Aussenstelle Dachau. In his new position Kick was charged with recruiting espionage agents from the Dachau Concentration Camp. He relied almost wholly on intimidating and coercive methods.

Suse, Edmund Theodor—Member Gestapo—Paris

Subject was brought to the attention of this detachment during the investigation and screening for the position of Assistant Mayor in Dachau. It was revealed that subject was interpreter for the Gestapo in Paris. Investigation in his house produced a list of party members from Allach, photographs of members of the NSDAP-Allach wearing the Golden Party pin (old fighters). His claims that he was in the SS Straflager could not be verified.

Lihotzky, Roland—Member Gestapo—Prague

Subject joined the NS student organization in Prague one month after the Germans had taken over on 26 April 1939. He was hired by Polizeirat Lustig, Gestapo Prague, in June 1939. He received 170 marks a month for his services, which consisted of translations, house searches and interpreting during interrogations. Subject claims that he was arrested 17 June 1940 in Prague for stealing soap and coffee. His case was heard January 1942 by RSHA-SS Sturmbannfuhrer Muller. Subject was subsequently sentenced to five years, three months, and was moved to the SS Straflager, Camp Dachau, 5 November 1942. In April 1943, he claims to have been made medical aid man in the SS prison. On 25 April 1945, three days before the Americans arrived, subject was issued a Red Cross armband.

Rechenberger

Subject tried to give information about the hideout of a minor SS member. He claims to have been in the SS Straflager for two and a half years when he left the RAD.[3] He has the SS blood group on his arm and could not be identified as having been in the SS Straflager. He was only known to two other arrested persons . . . Suse and Lihotzky. Since subject was not in the camp grounds but tried to get in voluntarily to give vague information, and since his story is obviously false, he is possibly an enemy agent.

Editor: Appendices A through D were a part of the report prepared by the CIC Detachment, Seventh Army. I have separated them and given each an appropriate title. This appendix retains its original title, "Special Case Reports."

---

3. Editor: RAD is the *Reichsarbeitsdienst* or State Labor Service. It required young adults to work in labor camps on public works projects and helped Hitler to reduce unemployment quite impressively.

B

The Political Department

The administration, supervision, and control of the Dachau Concentration Camp was divided into five departments:

- *Abteilung I—Kommandanture* (Commander of Camp and Personal Staff)

- *Abteilung II—Politische Abteilung* (Political Department)

- *Abteilung III—Schutzhaftlager* (The Internees' Camp)

- *Abteilung IV—Verwaltung* (Administration)

- *Abteilung V—Reviere* (Hospitals)

   The most important department, though it appears subordinate to the camp commander, was the Political Department. This department was under the command of Kick, Johann (*Kriminal Sekretar, SD Untersturmfuhrer*, Head of STAPO Aussenstelle in Dachau), who was in contact with Berlin, and it was this department's function to check and counter-check not only the camp commander's activities with the orders that the camp commander received from higher authorities, but to investigate the activities of all departments at Dachau.

   The chief function of the Political Department was to screen and process all political and other types of criminals, the keeping of their records, the notification of the higher interning authorities of deaths, discharges, or other disposition of the internees. Death sentences of internees were received by this department (from Berlin), and these sentences were referred for execution to *Abteilung III* (*Schutzhaftlager*), and upon the execution of the above, this department was responsible for turning in a final report of the carrying out of these orders.

Gestapo came from Munich to carry on interrogations at Dachau. It was the responsibility of this department to interrogate and abuse Russian prisoners of war who were brought here for that specific purpose. Orders for the inhumane interrogation of the Russian prisoners of war were carried out by this department.

Another function of this department was to recruit internees by intimidation for sabotage and espionage work.

Editor: Appendix B was a part of the report prepared by the CIC Detachment of the Seventh Army. It, along with the material in Appendices C and D, were originally entitled "Miscellaneous."

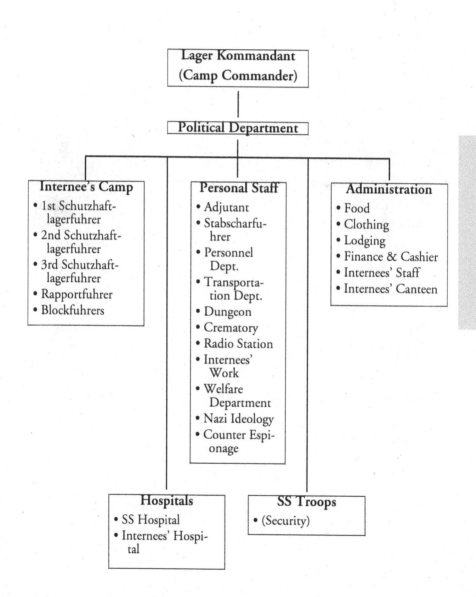

- **Lager Kommandant (Camp Commander)**
  - **Political Department**
    - **Internee's Camp**
      - 1st Schutzhaft-lagerfuhrer
      - 2nd Schutzhaft-lagerfuhrer
      - 3rd Schutzhaft-lagerfuhrer
      - Rapportfuhrer
      - Blockfuhrers
    - **Personal Staff**
      - Adjutant
      - Stabscharfu-hrer
      - Personnel Dept.
      - Transporta-tion Dept.
      - Dungeon
      - Crematory
      - Radio Station
      - Internees' Work
      - Welfare Department
      - Nazi Ideology
      - Counter Espionage
    - **Administration**
      - Food
      - Clothing
      - Lodging
      - Finance & Cashier
      - Internees' Staff
      - Internees' Canteen
    - **Hospitals**
      - SS Hospital
      - Internees' Hospital
    - **SS Troops**
      - (Security)

The International Prisoners Committee

President:

Patrick O'Leary....... Major ....England

Vice-President

Michailow, Nikolai ... General................. USSR

Haulot, Arthur .... Parliament Member.....Belgium

Members:

Kothbauer, Alfons .... Austria

Parra, Vincens................................. Spain

Michelet, Edmond .... France

Boellaard, Willem...........................Holland

Pallavicini, Georg......................... Hungary

Melodia, Giovanni .... Italy

Wirtz ....Luxemburg

Kokoszka, Josef.............................Poland

Blaha, Franz .... Czechoslovakia

Juranie, Oskar........................... Yugoslavia

Kuci, Ali.................................. Balkans

Jokarinis....................................Greece

Becker, Rasmus.............................Norway

Muller, Oscar .... Deutschland

Secretary

Malczewski, Leon

D

Dachau Statistics

Table 1: Dachau Internees by Nationality

Nationality	Number	Notes
German Nationals	1173	(incl. 6 women)
Belgians	848	
Danes	1	
British	8	
Estonians	11	
French	3918	
Greeks	195	
Italians	2184	
Croats	103	
Serbs	79	
Slovenes	2907	
Latianis	27	
Lithuianians	39	
Alsace Loraines	36	
Luxembourgers	133	
Dutch	558	
Norwegians	79	
Poles	9082	(incl. 96 women)
Rumanians	50	

Table 1: Dachau Internees by Nationality

Nationality	Number	Notes
Russians	4258	(incl. 9 women)
Slovaks	44	
Albanians	30	
Americans	6	
Maltese	1	
Arabians	1	
Armenians	2	
Finns	1	
Iraqs	1	
Irans	1	
Turks	3	
Spanish	194	
Exiles	21	
Czechs	1632	
Hungarians	670	(incl 34 women)
Bulgarians	8	
Portugese	4	
Swiss	2	
Austrians	253	
Annex-Germans	2	
Sudetens	3	
Jews	2539	(incl. 225 women)
Total	**31,432**	[incl. 370 women]

Number of Internees Processed Through Dachau

Table 2: Dachau Internees by Period

Period	Number of Internees
From 1933 to 1939 (Numbered card index system)	39,000
From 1933 to 1939 (Unnumbered cards)	21,000
From March 1940 to 26 April 1945 (From card index system established March 1940. Cards numbered from No. 1 and continued up to 26 April 1945)	161,930
Transports arriving 3 weeks prior to American occupation (No permanent records kept due to confusion and breakdown of the administrative departments during the attempted evacuation)	7,000
Total	228,930

Table 3: Natural Deaths at Dachau

1945 by Month	Deaths
January 1	3,800
February	3,200
March	3,700
April	4,000

Note: Compiled from card index system.

Executions

Table 4: Jewish Executions

Total number of Jews brought in from other concentration camps for executions from June 20, 1944 to November 23, 1944	29,138

Table 5: Non-Aliens (Germans from Foreign Countries)

Period	Number of Executions
1945, January, February, March	4861
1944	1987
1943	1108
1942	5194
1941	2898
1940 October, November, December	669
Total	**16,717**

Note: Partial figures compiled from accurate records. However, the most important and complete records of Dachau Concentration Camp were destroyed three weeks prior to American occupation.

Editor: In this appendix are four sets of statistics that were given separately in the original report in a section entitled "Survey of Internees at Dachau Concentration Camp by Nationalities at Liberation—29 April 1945."

Index

Printed in February 2023
by Rotomail Italia S.p.A., Vignate (MI) - Italy